LOCH NESS

UNCOVERED

LOCH NESS
UNCOVERED

**MEDIA, MISINFORMATION,
AND THE GREATEST
MONSTER HOAX
OF ALL TIME**

REBECCA SIEGEL

ASTRA YOUNG READERS

AN IMPRINT OF ASTRA BOOKS FOR YOUNG READERS
NEW YORK

Astra Young Readers
An imprint of Astra Books for Young Readers, a division of Astra Publishing House
astrapublishinghouse.com
Printed in the United States of America

ISBN: 978-1-6626-2023-2 (hc)
ISBN: 978-1-6626-2024-9 (eBook)

Library of Congress Cataloging-in-Publication Data
Names: Rissman, Rebecca, author.
Title: Loch Ness uncovered : how fake news fueled the greatest monster hoax
    of all time / by Rebecca Siegel.
Description: First edition. | New York : Astra Young Readers, an imprint of
    Astra Books for Young Readers, [2024] | Includes bibliographical
    references. | Audience: Ages 10 and up | Audience: Grades 7-9 | Summary:
    "Loch Ness Uncovered is an extensively researched, myth-busting account
    of the world's most famous monster hoax-the Loch Ness Monster-and a
    cautionary tale on the dangers of misinformation"— Provided by publisher.
Identifiers: LCCN 2023016602 (print) | LCCN 2023016603 (ebook) |
    ISBN 9781662620232 (hardcover) | ISBN 9781662620249 (epub)
Subjects: LCSH: Loch Ness monster"—Juvenile literature. |
    Legends"—Scotland"—Juvenile literature. | Monsters--Scotland--Juvenile
    literature. | Hoaxes"—Scotland"—History"—Juvenile literature. | Fake
    news"—Scotland"—History.
Classification: LCC QL89.2.L6 R57 2024 (print) | LCC QL89.2.L6 (ebook) |
    DDC 001.944"—dc23/eng/20230524
LC record available at https://lccn.loc.gov/2023016602
LC ebook record available at https://lccn.loc.gov/2023016603

First edition

10 9 8 7 6 5 4 3 2 1

Design by Red Herring Design
The text is set in ITC Esprit Book.
The titles are set in Bohemian Typewriter.

For the readers.
I believe in *you*.

CONTENTS

AUTHOR'S NOTE

Dear Reader,

Researching this book was the adventure of a lifetime. It began, as the best adventures do, in my hometown library. There, I peppered librarians with a growing list of requests: Do you have any books on Scottish folklore? Cryptids? Plesiosaurs? Golden Age Hollywood? Nazis? British media? After plowing my way through towering stacks of books, I turned to digital sources. I combed through online newspaper archives from the UK, America, Australia, and more, finding incredible details and realizing that two of the most important newspapers for this story, London's *Daily Mail* and the *Inverness Courier*, were unavailable in my area. If I wanted to get my hands on them, I needed to renew my passport.

In the summer of 2022, I took my library love affair abroad and traveled to London's legendary British Library. I spent days tucked away in its famous Newsroom, spooling fragile reels of newspaper microfilm onto fiddly knobs and delicately thumbing through aged, leatherbound books. I felt like the heroine in a mystery film, moments away from discovering some earth-shattering truth. I loved every second of it. The library in Inverness, Scotland, came next. Librarians there ushered me into a tiny, treasure-packed archive. A door was propped open to an empty workspace, and I spent days listening to rain hammer the roof and paging though hundreds of incredible monster history artifacts, taking breaks only for the occasional sausage roll or cream-slathered scone. I flipped through one book that was the size of my kitchen table and another that was the size of a deck of cards. Librarians occasionally popped in to say hello or suggest a resource, but I was largely on my own to read, explore, and imagine. It was heaven.

As much as I adore them, libraries facilitated only part of my research. I also spent hours outside of their hallowed walls, talking to a wide range of experts who helped me understand the many parts of this story. I talked to a retired CIA analyst about what fake news means. I interviewed a psychologist about biases, and I asked a vision science professor at MIT about the mechanics of monster sightings. I talked to monster hunters and monster skeptics. I had coffee with Peter Wetherell, the descendent of Marmaduke and Ian Wetherell, and breakfast with a man known as "Mr. Loch Ness." I got to know the former NASA Jet Propulsion Laboratory engineer who enhanced images of Nessie back in the 1970s, and I sat on a little wooden bench with the director of the Loch Ness Centre, Adrian Shine. Each of these interactions added a layer of understanding and depth to this story. These generous people told riveting stories, answered my questions, and, in one case, let me peek into an active archaeological dig. I can't tell you how much I loved this part of the process.

Of course, no research into the story of the Loch Ness Monster could be complete without going on an actual monster hunt. So, on one particularly cloudy morning, I pulled on a warm sweater, slid into my rain gear, and climbed aboard a small sonar-equipped boat on Loch Ness. By this point in my journey, I knew just about everything there was to know about this tale. I knew the people, the hoaxes, and the scandals. I knew the science, the history, and the geography. I knew there was no monster. Still, sitting on the water, I felt unsettled. The area is spooky. It's remote and quiet. Ruins of a crumbling castle cling to one coast. Forested hillsides on either side of the loch scramble up toward the sky, as if trying to escape its grasp. But the strangest part of Loch Ness is the water itself. It's ink black. As our boat puttered out into the center of the loch that morning, I couldn't stop myself from staring at the water. I leaned over the metal rails and gazed down at its mirrorlike surface, wanting desperately to see what lurked beneath but seeing only my own reflection.

It was the perfect metaphor for this story. *Loch Ness Uncovered* isn't about what's under the water. It's about the people above the surface and the stories they tell.

Happy reading,
Rebecca Siegel

CHAPTER 1

BEGINNINGS

There was a beast in Loch Ness. Aldie Mackay delivered this shocking bit of information on April 14, 1933, her lilting Scottish accent wrapping around each strange detail.

Earlier that day, she and her husband John had been taking a drive along the loch's northern coast. It was a pleasant day. Clouds speckled the blue sky. The loch's surface looked perfectly still. Suddenly, a violent commotion in the water caught her attention. Some kind of animal was thrashing on the surface. Foam and spray shot into the air. The creature soon stopped splashing, but it didn't disappear. Two glistening humps appeared above the surface. They had the deep blue-black coloring of a whale, and were large and widely spaced, hinting at a giant creature below. The humps undulated across the water, rising and falling in a snakelike manner. And then, just as quickly as it had appeared, the creature dove back beneath the surface. The water stilled. Mackay turned to her husband, who had only just brought their vehicle to a stop. He hadn't seen the creature at all.

Stunned, the pair sat in their car for thirty minutes. They stared at the water, hoping that the animal might make a second appearance. When it didn't, they made their way to the

The Drumnadrochit Hotel

Drumnadrochit Hotel, a stately establishment they managed together. There, Mackay shared her story.

Listeners must have been baffled, shocked. At the time, Loch Ness had no uniquely frightening reputation. It was simply one of many quiet, picturesque lakes in the Scottish Highlands. Ferries regularly chugged along its twenty-three-mile length, while small boats zipped back and forth across its narrow one-and-a-half-mile width. Its shorelines were mostly undeveloped, save for the occasional country home, castle, or medieval ruin. Other than its impressive depth, which dropped down to 788 feet at its deepest point, the most remarkable thing about the loch was the color of its water. Loch Ness was as black as night. Scotland's frequent rains had washed eons of peat down the surrounding hillsides and into the loch, causing it to be nearly opaque. Mackay's claim about a huge, humped beast in Loch Ness was the first of its kind.

In addition to shock, some listeners may have also felt a twinge of doubt hearing Mackay's tale. She was the sole witness to this unusual event. Neither her husband nor any other locals could verify her account. She also appeared to be ignoring a simple explanation for the commotion: a pair of seals may have just gotten themselves into the loch. But perhaps most importantly, Mackay had a personal motive for sharing such an intriguing tale. She had a loch side hotel to keep afloat.

In truth, the most frightening thing locals had witnessed in recent years was a general decline in tourism. Loch Ness had previously enjoyed nearly two centuries as a favorite destination for wealthy British travelers. They came to the peaceful, dark loch to enjoy a break from the hubbub of aristocratic life. After the royal family made their way to Loch Ness, with Prince Albert visiting in 1847 and Queen Victoria following in 1873, the loch's status as a high-end getaway was sealed. At one point, extra ferries even had to be added to accommodate the water traffic, and a special train line was built to help usher visitors to the place advertised as "a most interesting and romantic part of the Highlands." -But eventually the loch's sparkling appeal dulled. The train line closed. The ferries slowed. By 1933, the area had settled into a quiet rhythm. Making things worse, that season's fishing output had been less productive than usual. A newspaper called the area's herring haul "very poor and practically disastrous."-Another observer labeled it "lamentably" bad. The area needed a boost.

Under normal circumstances, Mackay's claim might have been shared, lightly debated, and then forgotten. She may have even laughed and shrugged the whole thing off, chalking it up to a trick of the light or an overactive imagination. But circumstances weren't normal. Mackay happened to tell her story in a time and place uniquely primed for an extraordinary event. Science, art, and culture were changing so rapidly that anything seemed possible. The stars were aligned for a strange little tale to grow in size and importance. Then something happened that launched Mackay's story into the stratosphere. The press got involved.

Alex Campbell was a freelance writer for a local paper called the *Inverness Courier*. When he heard of Mackay's odd sighting, he recognized its appeal and made quick work of writing it up for publication. In the tradition of so many journalists at the time, Campbell made little effort to stick to the facts. Rather, he took an already odd tale and embellished it. He included fictional details and emotionally provocative language, declined to name Mackay in the story, and also remained anonymous himself, identifying only as "a correspondent."

Alex Campbell's article in the *Inverness Courier*, printed May 2, 1933.

STRANGE SPECTACLE ON LOCH NESS

What was it?

(FROM A CORRESPONDENT)

Loch Ness has for generations been credited with being the home of a fearsome-looking monster, but, somehow or other, the "water-kelpie," as this legendary creature is called, has always been regarded as a myth, if not a joke. Now, however, comes the news that the beast has been seen once more, for, on Friday of last week, a well-known business man, who lives near Inverness, and his wife (a University graduate), when motoring along the north shore of the loch, not far from Abriachan Pier, were startled to see a tremendous upheaval on the loch, which, previously, had been as calm as the proverbial mill-pond. The lady was the first to notice the disturbance, which occurred fully three-quarters of a mile from the shore, and it was her sudden cries to stop that drew her husband's attention to the water.

There, the creature disported itself, rolling and plunging for fully a minute, its body resembling that of a whale, and the water cascading and churning like a simmering cauldron. Soon, however, it disappeared in a boiling mass of foam. Both onlookers confessed that there was something uncanny about the whole thing, for they realised that here was no ordinary denizen of the depths, because, apart from its enormous size, the beast, in taking the final plunge, sent out waves that were big enough to have been caused by a passing steamer. The watchers waited for almost half-an-hour in the hope that the monster (if such it was) would come to the surface again; but they had seen the last of it. Questioned as to the length of the beast, the lady stated that, judging by the state of the water in the affected area, it seemed to be many foot long.

It will be remembered that a few years ago, a party of Inverness anglers reported that when crossing the loch in a rowing-boat, they encountered an unknown creature, whose bulk, movements, and the amount of water it displaced at once suggested that it was either a very large seal, a porpoise, or, indeed, the monster itself.

But the story, which duly appeared in the press, received scant attention and less credence. In fact, most of those people who aired their views on the matter did so in a manner that bespoke feelings of the utmost scepticism.

It should be mentioned that, so far as is known, neither seals or porpoises have ever been known to enter Loch Ness. Indeed, in the case of the latter, it would be utterly impossible for them to do so, and, as to the seals, it is a fact that though they have on rare occasions been seen in the River Ness, their presence in Loch Ness has never once been definitely established.

His misinformation-filled column hit newsstands on May 2, 1933, both setting a standard for the way future journalists would handle Loch Ness Monster reporting, and shocking the public at the same time.

"Strange Spectacle on Loch Ness: What Was It?" informed readers that a *monster* lived in Loch Ness. And not just any monster, but a large, "fearsome-looking," whale-like beast. Campbell declared that Mackay's sighting wasn't some shocking new revelation, but confirmation of a generations-old belief. His column made it seem as though locals had always been on the lookout for such an aquatic creature.

The stage was set for the drama of the century. Loch Ness had itself a monster.

Alex Campbell

Marmaduke Wetherell

CHAPTER 2

WANDERLUST

As Scottish Highlanders pondered the likelihood of a monster in Loch Ness, British theatergoers gaped at a different type of water beast altogether: the African hippo. This huge and deadly monster was just one of the stars of Marmaduke Wetherell's newest film, *Wanderlust*.

At fifty, Wetherell was a wrinkled, bushy-browed, swashbuckling showman with an eye for drama. And *Wanderlust* delivered plenty of drama. Audiences gazed in rapt attention at the black-and-white film's documentary-style footage of animals in Africa, including stalking leopards, grazing buffalo, lumbering hippos, and giraffes with impossibly long limbs. They tittered nervously at footage of a lion swatting at a crew member and gasped in horror at the destruction caused by a plague of locusts. Wetherell had done a fine job not only of filming a variety of wildlife but also in presenting it. His movie was easy to follow, entertaining, and occasionally even funny. Critics called it "excellent."

Wetherell's success with *Wanderlust* was hard earned. He'd spent decades trying to make a name for himself as an actor, appearing everywhere from cramped London playhouses to the silver screen. When success didn't hit in England, he traveled to

British-controlled South Africa to try his luck there. He appeared in several African Film Productions movies. Still, fame remained just out of reach.

Wetherell's ambitions weren't limited to the world of theater. He tried other things, too, splitting his time between England, South Africa, and Northern Rhodesia (now Zambia). There were the years he tried to become a farmer in Northern Rhodesia, a plan he ultimately abandoned when the farm had "bust up." And there were the years he'd put into academics, toying with both anthropology and zoology. He tromped across the English countryside in search of ancient ruins and through the African veldt stalking animals. His accomplishments in both fields were respectable but minor. Eventually, Wetherell worked as a big game hunting guide for wealthy British tourists, too. He kept his clients safe and happy but he was otherwise unremarkable at the job. He still hadn't found his niche.

In 1925, Wetherell came tantalizingly close to cinematic success with a film called *Livingstone*. Wetherell wrote, directed, and starred in the epic biopic, which told the story of David Livingstone, an explorer, missionary, and abolitionist. Livingstone had famously traveled through regions of southern, eastern, and central Africa. Wetherell chose to film most of the scenes on-site, in the very places Livingstone had been. This was a massive undertaking. Wetherell's team spent their days swatting at thieving baboons and stepping over thirteen-foot-long pythons. They tracked elusive lions on epic, days-long, silent chases. Once, a herd of stampeding buffalo nearly trampled Wetherell's crew, who managed to escape by scrambling to the top of ten-foot-high anthills. Another time, a band of irritated hippos followed his group down a river. The huge beasts periodically rammed their fragile boats in an attempt to knock the film crew into the water. The *Livingstone* team was scratched by razor grass, bitten by tsetse flies, burned by the sun, and soaked by frigid mountain rain. The filming process left Wetherell so ravaged that he became unrecognizable. "Please excuse the peculiar appearance of my face," he told a startled onlooker mid-production. "It is in the cause of art."

After two long years of work, *Livingstone* premiered in British theaters. It was a box office flop. Viewers liked the film, and critics gave it pleasantly lukewarm reviews, but it didn't bring in the expected cash. By all outward appearances, Wetherell had missed the mark yet again. But in truth, *Livingstone* had actually uncovered Wetherell's greatest skill: storytelling. All throughout the filming process, he had regaled people with stories of the film's production—of the miles and miles he traveled on foot, of the lions he'd spotted and hunted, and of the crocodiles he'd evaded. Listeners hung on his every word, and it wasn't long before newspapers got in on the game. Publications, like London's *Sunday Post*, delighted their readers with tales from the "Man of Many Parts," who had seen more of Africa than most Brits could even imagine.

Wetherell kept his stories short and splashy. He highlighted the events that would be most interesting and ignored the details that were dull. In this way, Wetherell was able to use the newspapers and magazines as an extension of his art.

Livingstone might not have been a cinematic showstopper, but it catapulted Wetherell into the public consciousness as a storyteller. As the years passed and he continued making movies, he maintained his relationship with the press. When he filmed his 1927 *Robinson Crusoe* on-site in Tobago, he once again delighted editors and readers alike with fantastic behind-the-scenes tales. Readers of the *Sphere* were even treated to a photo spread of Wetherell at work, walking on the sand, eyeing an assortment of rifles, and wading into hip-high water while holding a sea turtle. By the time *Wanderlust* premiered in 1933, audiences knew what to expect of Wetherell. He was going to give them a dramatic story filled with wild animals. What no one yet knew was that Wetherell would soon deliver the world its wildest animal story ever.

But first, the Loch Ness Monster needed to make a few more waves.

CHAPTER 3

MONSTER SIGHTINGS

On a crisp, sunny day in May 1933, four men gathered along the rocky shoreline of Loch Ness. They stared at the loch's glassy surface with a variety of expressions: bored, expectant, and curious. One man pointed a long, thin telescope toward the water and held it up to his eye. The "beastie" in the loch could show up at any moment.

Following the article about Aldie Mackay's alleged monster encounter, interest in the reclusive beast steadily grew. People couldn't stop talking about what newspapers were calling a "sea monster," "mystery monster," or simply, the "Loch Ness Monster." Some reacted to the chilling story with doubt. Others were curious. Plenty were downright inspired. They crept down the loch's shores, eager but also afraid.

Within weeks, some of these intrepid monster hunters had incredible news. They'd seen the beast, too! Local journalists jumped at the chance to report on the stories. Much as Alex Campbell had done in his first column on the beast, these journalists sprinkled their columns with unreliable information. Sensational language dripped from the newsprint, as did outlandish details. They informed readers that monster witnesses ranged from school children to respected adults. On May 23, the *Dundee Courier* noted that a local man who had "previously disbelieved" in the monster, spotted the beast himself. In his excitement, he'd called his son and friend over, and the trio watched the beast for a full ten minutes through a telescope. A week later, the monster appeared to startled passengers on board a local bus. Observers tried their best to estimate its size, and their guesses were jaw-dropping. The beast was a whopper, likely somewhere between twenty- and thirty-feet long.

Tourism around the loch boomed. Folks from throughout Scotland and England made a beeline for the dark waters, desperate to catch a glimpse of tail or fin. Steamship cruises along its waters became "very popular, both with visitors and residents." The *Courier* even warned tourists not to get onto a boat without the proper equipment: "When cruising, take a camera." It would be a shame to miss the chance to photograph the beast.

In June, local newspapers published more monster sightings. One described how a group of workmen excavating a hillside near Abriachan were "startled to see the monster in the center of the loch," swimming closely behind a cruising boat. They noted that the beast pursued the boat for "some distance" and observed several striking characteristics, including "an enormous head and a large, heavy body." Another sighting was reportedly so "unpleasant and exciting" that it caused a boating woman to faint.

Guesses about the beast's identity, characteristics, and behavior floated above the loch's black surface. Uncertainty reigned. Part of this had to do with the fact that the early ideas of the Loch Ness Monster varied wildly from person to person. Some thought of the monster as a giant, wriggling, eellike beast. Others pictured a bulbous creature with a big head and a broad, rounded body. Still others figured it looked distinctly horselike. Despite all the ambiguity, one thing was clear: this wave of monster sightings had transformed Loch Ness from a sleepy spot in the Scottish Highlands into a mysterious, captivating, enchanted place.

As spring faded into summer, an observer gazed out over the loch near the medieval ruins of Urquhart Castle. The black water stretched endlessly to the east and west. Boats trawled lazily across its wind-rippled surface. White seagulls swooped noisily overhead. And then, in a breath, the whole scene became bathed in technicolor when a giant rainbow formed across the loch. Vivid reds, purples, yellows, blues, and greens suddenly hung in the air, casting a candy-colored filter onto the watery scene. It was exquisite and unreal, as though the loch had been touched by magic.

Anyone reading the papers might believed that it had indeed.

CHAPTER 4

ABOMINATION

Georph Spicer held his Austin convertible at a steady 20 miles per hour as he and his wife, Lilian, made a slow and pleasant trek through the Scottish Highlands. It was July 22, 1933, and the pair were enjoying a peaceful summer afternoon, en route home from a vacation in the North Country.

Spicer, fifty-seven, was a London tailor who made people think of words like "quiet" and "retiring." His face was kind, if slightly mousy, with small, dark eyes and pronounced cheekbones. His hairline crept back from his forehead as if to say, "after you, sir." Spicer described himself as "temperate," which is a perfectly proper word for boring. Few historical records exist for his wife, Lilian, save for her occasional appearances at London weddings and funerals. She was a polite, middle-class British woman and therefore stayed home as a housewife. Together, the Spicers appeared to be respectable and unremarkable.

On one side of the Spicers' convertible, a green, forested hillside climbed up into the sky, speckled with flowers and outcroppings of gray stone. On the other side of their car, the landscape tumbled away into the gray-black waters of a lake that had recently begun to enjoy quite a bit of notoriety: Loch Ness.

Rumors about the loch's mysterious beast ran rampant. Locals debated the various stories' merits, and tourists gaped at the water. It was the beginning of a phase later called "Loch Ness Monster Fever," when the beast seemed to always be on people's minds. Though the Spicers' route took them directly through this storm of interest, the pair would later state that they

George Spicer

knew nothing of the monster chatter as they took their pleasant, slow drive around the loch. This made what happened next all the more shocking. *The Spicers claimed that they saw the monster cross the road.*

On August 4, the *Inverness Courier* broadcast this development in a column that included a letter from Spicer himself. He reported that he'd seen a giant creature lurch across the road at the crest of a hill, about fifty yards in front of his vehicle. It was about "six feet to eight feet" in length, with a "long neck," a "fairly big" body, and a "high back." He hadn't been able to see the feet or tail because of his position on the road below it, but he noted that it moved in an odd, jerky fashion as it crossed from the left side of the road to the right. He said the beast was "very ugly," and that it was the "nearest approach to a dragon or pre-historic animal" that he'd ever seen. Interestingly, the quiet tailor hadn't been particularly afraid of this ghastly beast. He even boasted that if he'd been any nearer to it, he might have "tackled it."

The letter ended with an ominous declaration about the monster. "There is no doubt that it exists."

This entire story was staggering, not just for the fact that Spicer said he had just seen a *monster*, though of course that was a thrill. It was important primarily for the fact that Spicer said his beast had been on *land*. Before this, newspaper stories about the Loch Ness Monster only reported that it had been seen in the water. People had seen splashing or darkened ripples. They'd seen wake or froth. But a huge beast lumbering across the road? That was something new. Spicer's story was additionally significant because of the way he described the creature. Previous sightings had compared the beast to familiar water-dwelling animals—eels, sturgeon, seals, or porpoises. Things with fins and tails. Or, witnesses had suggested human-made explanations for what they'd seen, such as an upturned boat. No one up until this point had suggested that the monster looked anything like a dragon or prehistoric creature.

After the *Inverness Courier* printed his story, other publications reported on it as well. Readers gaped at the update. This monster business just kept getting better!

A few months after his reported sighting, George Spicer churned out a shaky sketch of what he'd seen. It had a big, rounded body and a long, snaking neck. It looked like a terribly drawn long-necked dinosaur. In fact, it strongly resembled a long-necked dinosaur that had only just had its silver screen debut in the new box office smash, *King Kong*.

CHAPTER 5

KONG

As Loch Ness Monster fever descended upon the Scottish Highlands, a new movie called *King Kong* was captivating audiences from Los Angeles to London. The film's plot was improbable at best: a giant ape who lives on an island full of warring dinosaurs falls in lust with a relentlessly shrieking actress in a blonde wig. General chaos ensues and Kong winds up at the top of the Empire State Building, swatting at annoying fighter planes. The planes pepper him with bullets until finally, finally, he falls to his death. For the modern viewer, the movie is hard to swallow. Its storyline is shaky and racist; its acting over the top. But 1933 audiences couldn't get enough.

King Kong was a special effects bonanza. Theatergoers gaped at scenes of "Skull Island," a tropical place populated by a cast of hungry, extinct creatures. There was a pterodactyl, a stegosaurus, and a tyrannosaurus. But the dinosaurs were nothing compared to the star himself. Kong was a furry, towering brute, with eyebrows that waggled and muscles that quivered. As he stomped across the screen, squashing one unfortunate chap beneath his foot or popping another into his gaping maw, theatergoers resorted to nervous giggling. They were unsure whether to feel scared, delighted, or both.

Model ape from the 1933 film, *King Kong*

Kong was the product of Hollywood special effects visionary, Willis O'Brien. He used a technique called stop-motion photography to transform small, movable models into giant, living, breathing monsters. This meticulous process involved posing a model creature in front of a camera and shooting a single frame. Next, an animator would make a tiny change to the model's position—lifting an arm a millimeter or shifting an eyebrow ever so subtly, before shooting another frame. It was painstaking. The lighting had to be consistent, the models kept in pristine condition. Some scenes of the movie required 150 hours of work for a single minute of film. Fortunately, O'Brien's work paid off. A critic at the *Sunday Mirror* told readers that the movie's "aim is to make your eyes pop out of your head, and it succeeds beyond all my expectations."

Though the starring players in *King Kong* were an ape and his human love interest, it was another creature who had the biggest impact on the world. This monster appeared about halfway through the film, just as a troupe of high-trousered sailors set out into the jungle. They board a makeshift wooden raft and begin crossing a dark, foggy pond. The scene is tense. Once the sailors reach the center of the pond, a giant, glistening head breaks the surface. Water drips off its ghastly snout. It's a dinosaur! An awful, dagger-toothed, bloodthirsty brontosaurus! The men, seemingly unaware that real brontosauruses were plant eaters, fire pistols and rifles wildly at the monster. Chaos erupts. The dinosaur ducks below the water before quickly surfacing again, upsetting the raft and sending its passengers toppling into the water. The brontosaurus scoops up unfortunate sailors and starts to clumsily chomp on them. The surviving men scramble to the shore and flee through the jungle. The dinosaur gives chase, and the viewer is treated to a spectacular vision of the beast in profile as it marches after its prey. It crosses the screen from left to right, displaying its large, barrel-shaped body, long neck, and small head. Its legs and dragging tail aren't visible due to the thick jungle foliage. As it moves, its head jerks forward on its long neck.

The brontosaurus's appearance had a profound impact on moviegoers, including a stuffy British tailor named George Spicer. Sure enough, Spicer had recently watched *King Kong*.

The similarities between Spicer's monster and the long-necked dinosaur in *King Kong* were clear. The beasts' shape, behavior, and movement were near-perfect matches. One newspaper picked up on the connection, headlining an article about the monster:

"Not From King Kong's Isle." This emphasized just how extraordinary the tales coming out of Loch Ness really were. People were seeing a creature fit for a horror movie. Modern cryptid researchers Daniel Loxton and Donald R. Prothero think it went a bit further than that. The pair believe that Spicer didn't just see a creature fit for *King Kong*. He saw the creature *from King Kong*. They argue that Spicer's long-necked monster was "lifted right off of *King Kong*'s Skull Island." This would have been a frightening and surprising ordeal. And it was exactly the sort of thing social scientists had been warning about.

In the years leading up to Spicer's sighting, cinema had become incredibly popular. England in the 1930s was home to more than five thousand movie theaters. About 40 percent of

King Kong's fearsome brontosaurus

the population attended movies at least once a week. Movies were all the rage and, for a certain group of hand-wringing researchers, that was absolutely terrifying. Cinema presented audiences with all sorts of lewd ideas. Kissing! Fighting! More kissing! But beyond all that, cinema seemed to immerse people in new environments a little too convincingly. Ticket holders would walk into a theater and be whisked to another world. Some scientists feared that this immersive experience might addle some brains. Theatergoers might begin to confuse what was real with what was not, dragging the imaginary movie world along with them into their regular lives. The same year that *King Kong* hit theaters, film researcher Herbert Blumer dove into this very topic. He noticed that "many people" walked around, "carry[ing] a movie world in their heads." Blumer interviewed theatergoers and nabbed dozens of terrifying quotes about the ways movies had impacted them. One confessed that "movies gave me a lot of foolish ideas which my imagination accepted as facts." Cinema wasn't just a newfangled form of entertainment; it was a harmful medium that could lead to mass confusion. For Spicer, that prediction certainly seemed to ring true. He appeared to be so caught up in his own cinematic recollections that he *thought* he saw a monster cross the road that day.

George Spicer and *King Kong* gave the world a rough outline for the Loch Ness Monster. She was a large, long-necked, dragon-like beast. Next, the press needed to fill in the details.

CHAPTER 6

SILLY SEASON

George Spicer's monster sighting took place just as an odd phenomenon chugged to life in newspaper rooms around the world. This strange period, which has occurred each year since the mid-1800s and lasts from July until September, has different names in different countries. The British and Americans call it silly season. In Sweden, it's the *nyhetstorka* (news drought), and it's *la morte-saison* (the dead season) in France. Germans equate the season with a popular late summer snack, so they call it *Sauregurkenzeit* (pickled gherkin time). The stories that appear during silly season often have their own name. Spaniards call them *serpientes de verano* (summer snakes) because of their tendency to writhe endlessly on, while Finns call them *mätäkuun jutut* (rotting month stories). Silly season happens when major political organizations take long summer breaks causing an annual lull in news. Parliament goes on recess, as does Congress. Individual party leaders embark on lazy summer vacations. This means that political news stories dry up, leaving writers with empty pages and looming deadlines. During silly season, columns normally filled with important updates on things like laws and the economy are filled with sensational, humorous, and bizarre tales.

In the early 1900s, silly season stories informed the public about everything from a man who declared himself the world's "sit-in-a-floating-barrel champion" to a woman who breastfed a wild bear. It was a free-for-all. Some silly season news stories were deliberately misleading or false. Others were simply filled with errors. Misinformation ran rampant.

Though silly seasons in the 1930s presented readers with an ever-changing cast of characters, there was one guest star who enjoyed a recurring role: the sea serpent. Each year during silly season, sea serpent stories poured in to papers. And publishers, eager for copy, printed them. They told of ship captains spotting giant snakelike beasts under the waves, or sailors cowering at mysterious shadows beneath the water. It was such an expected phenomenon that some people even referred to silly season as sea serpent season. As a *Chicago Tribune* writer put it, "When all the world is so quiet that the cable editor has nothing to do . . . then the sea serpent arises in his horrendous majesty."

When George Spicer's Loch Ness Monster sighting was printed on August 4, 1933, it kicked off the ultimate silly sea serpent season. Within days, monster sighting stories began spilling onto local newspapers. A maid named Nellie Smith came forward to report that she'd spent a terrifying ten minutes staring at the beast as it swam in huge, lazy circles in the loch. Days later, another maid named Prudence Keyes claimed a sighting of her own, noting that she'd also spotted the monster swimming laps. Word of Keyes' sighting spread to the nearby house of Royal Navy Engineer Commander R. Meiklem, sending its inhabitants sprinting to the windows. They, too, claimed they were lucky enough to witness the monster. Commander Meiklem later reported his sighting to the *Dundee Courier*, explaining that the creature was "quite as big as a horse." It had a "sharply rising peak-shaped back" that "seemed to be dotted with knobbly lumps," and was "black or a very dark brown" in color. Commander Meiklem appeared rattled by the incident. He told the *Courier* that "in all his experience at home or abroad he had never seen anything like it before."

This flood of stories influenced the way people looked at the loch. When a Mrs. Cheshire spotted "a big black object in the water," she first assumed it was simply "a piece of shining rock." It wasn't until later—after she'd had the chance to reflect on the incident and discuss it with neighbors—that she changed her tune. She'd seen the beast! Days later, the *Inverness Courier* told readers that Cheshire had officially joined the club of monster viewers.

Local Scottish papers kept the monster stories coming through the end of August. They reported that a pair of sisters, Mrs. MacDonnell and Mrs. Sutherland were standing on the loch's rocky shoreline when a strange, flatheaded creature broke the surface. It was only one hundred yards away, giving them front row seats to the show. The women's close proximity to the animal apparently allowed them to see incredible details, which journalists gladly passed along to their readers. The monster was huge. It looked to be about thirty feet long, with a "'wriggly neck.'" It had moved in "much the same way as a snake propels itself," slithering across the water. They noted the time of day (between 9:00 a.m. and 10:00 a.m.) and weather conditions (sunny). The loch had been very still, thus allowing a clear view of its monstrous guest. Details like these painted a vivid picture for newspaper readers.

Silly season normally wraps up in September, but the stories coming out of Loch Ness didn't slow down as the summer of

1933 faded into fall. Instead, they swirled in a waterlogged feedback loop. Sightings were claimed, reported, and read. Then more sightings were claimed, reported, and read. On and on it went. People saw the monster from all corners of the loch, at different times of day, and under different conditions. The monster reports came so fast and frequently that they were often jumbled together in the press, with one sighting referencing another.

Villages around Loch Ness hummed with activity. The narrow, winding roads clogged with tourist traffic. Trains through the Highlands were overcrowded. Newsrooms, too, buzzed excitedly as reporters scrambled to take down each new sighting. A respected minister saw the monster, as did a policeman's son. Women saw it, men saw it, and children saw it, too. One person even *heard* the Loch Ness Monster. He said the beast had issued a loud cough as it surfaced.

The desire to spot the beast took some folks to impressive heights. Charles Lindbergh, the world's most famous aviator, and his wife Anne flew over the loch in October. Anne later remembered the "great excitement in Inverness about some 'big beastie' in the loch." She and her husband were sternly warned, "Don't shoot the monster of Loch Ness." Plenty of lesser-known pilots also gave the loch a curious peek. In December, an industrious film crew chartered an aircraft and zipped overhead, cameras held at the ready. Unfortunately, all they managed to spot were a few "strangely shaped floating objects" on its surface. They hesitantly acknowledged that some people might have confused these objects for the monster, a suggestion that was both logical and also deeply unexciting.

Being skeptical of the Loch Ness Monster's existence wasn't a very fun position to take. It felt stodgy, boring, and unimaginative.

However, plenty of people found themselves firmly on this side of the issue. While droves of monster lovers squinted into the water, desperate for a sighting of their own, disbelievers spent just as much effort searching for rational explanations. They pointed to animals that could be mistaken for the monster, such as birds, fish, otters, and seals. They reminded anyone who would listen that those creatures could—under the right circumstances—resemble a monster. They also suggested other objects, like overturned boats and tree stumps, which could easily have looked like a curved back or bent neck.

Some of the more vocal skeptics wrote letters to their newspapers asserting their doubts about the monster. Editors gladly sent them to press, knowing that the only thing better than a wild story was a wildly controversial one. These letters ranged from polite ("I am of the opinion that it is a large grey seal") to odd ("it may be" a "horse"). Some were downright exasperated. It was a matter of "mistaken observation," wrote one beleaguered cynic, who noted that any other explanation was "improbable or absurd."

A well-known boat captain named John Macdonald wrote to the *Inverness Courier* with a string of objections to the idea of a monster in the loch. He said he'd sailed the loch for fifty years and had never seen, nor even heard of, a monster in its depths. He argued that people were just seeing shoals of salmon rushing the surface. And he reminded readers that the government had only recently surveyed the whole loch in a detailed, three-year-long project. Workers had scoured every inch of the water, sounding its every corner and inlet. Yet "nothing in the way of abnormal fish or beasts" had been spotted. Macdonald concluded his letter with a quick apology for ruining everyone's fun, noting that he didn't want to "kill a good yarn that adds to the romance of the beautiful loch."

In November, a knobbly log was hauled out of the loch that looked suspiciously like Commander Meiklem's monster. The cynics rejoiced. Perhaps the "monster" was just a log all along! They smiled at the idea that the monster nonsense would finally come to an end. But monster believers weren't convinced. They ignored the log as a coincidence and kept their eyes trained on the loch, as entertained as if they were watching a sports match.

Realizing monster believers couldn't be reasoned with, some skeptics tried another method for tamping out monster fever: ridicule. They made fun of monster lovers, suggesting that people who claimed to have seen it were suggestible, foolish, or just plain drunk. The fact that the monster was in Scotland, the birthplace of the highly alcoholic spirit, scotch, was just too tempting a punchline for many. Famed comedian, Sir Harry Lauder, put a spin on a famous Robert Burns poem for a newspaper called *John Bull*:

"[If] a body spy a body
Bathing in the Ness,
Need a body rush to tell
The laddies of the Press
That he's seen a Monster there,
All red in tooth and claw,
Fiercer far than any that
Poor Tam O' Shanter saw?

[If] a body meet a body
Coming by the Loch,

Often it will gie a body
Quite a muckle shock;
It may be a bonnie lassie,
But she won't look such
To a body who has had
A wee drap owermuch!"

Though skeptics like Lauder made entertaining and convincing cases against the existence of a monster, the excitement
and possibility of the alternative won out. The idea that there
could be a monster in the water was too thrilling to discount.
Believers soldiered on in their quest to spot the beast. For some
enthusiastic monster lovers, a sighting wasn't enough. They
wanted more.

By the end of 1933, multiple organized monster hunts were
underway. One was led by a local group of fishermen who didn't
like the idea of a monster in their waters, especially if it disrupted
their fishing. Anything that impacted their yearly haul would
have to go. The joint clerk to the Ness District fishery board,
Mr. Athole Mackintosh, vowed that if the beast, or the noisy
tourists chasing it, hurt the fish populations in the slightest, his
group would take whatever action was necessary to "protect
the great shoals of salmon" there. He didn't spell it out, but the
implication was clear. They'd kill the monster before it killed
their trade.

Another group of monster hunters attempted to commission
a forty-foot-long steel cage from metalworkers in Glasgow,
along with steel netting that they'd use to "dredge" the loch for
the monster. The Glaswegian metalworkers refused to take the
job, noting that the monster hunters hadn't organized a plan to

Steelworkers craft a monster cage, 1933.

transport the giant cage to the Highlands, and also that the metalworkers considered the whole thing a joke. Other workers were apparently less critical of the plan. They were soon spotted constructing a huge metal cage fit for the beast.

The Loch Ness Monster might have been what one historian has called "the best silly season story of all time," but some people weren't laughing about these plans to kill or capture the monster. They liked their strange, reclusive beast and wanted to keep it safe. A Sussex fisherman put out a desperate call for help. He said that without proper protection, the monster was "fair game for Tom, Dick or Harry, armed with a rifle." A member of Parliament named Sir Murdoch Macdonald read about these concerns. Macdonald could see how valuable the monster was. He said that as long as the beast wasn't "really dangerous in the ordinary sense, then it was the finest advertisement the Highlands have ever had." As such, it needed to be protected. Macdonald didn't like the idea of some "fool" taking a shot at Scotland's monster. He said anyone guilty of such a crime ought to be "hanged, drawn, and quartered."

Macdonald passed the issue up the chain of command. He wrote a letter to the Scottish secretary of state, Sir Godfrey Collins, stating that "the evidence of [the monster's] presence can be taken as undoubted." He asked Collins to bring a bill to Parliament that would guarantee the beast's protection. This put Collins in a bit of a bind, since there wasn't exactly a legal precedent in place for dealing with giant lake beasts. His advisors told him that there was "no law for the protection of 'monsters,'" and that his best bet was to ask local police to interpret existing laws in a way that would help the monster. For example, they might lean on laws forbidding trespassing as a way to discourage hunters from tromping along the shoreline. Collins agreed to this plan. Days later, Scottish papers reported that there were five police officers stationed around the loch.

Scottish people had good reason to feel protective of their monster. It was an absolute cash cow.

enough work to feed

CHAPTER 7

MONEY

On December 12, 1933, Scotland's Secretary of State, Sir Godfrey Collins, faced an unusual question. Standing beneath the towering ceiling of Britain's House of Commons, and surrounded by some of the most important men in the United Kingdom, the politician weighed his options. He'd just been asked whether the Royal Air Force should be called upon to observe and photograph the Loch Ness Monster. Collins managed to hold it together long enough to issue a stiff response: No. No, he would not be calling upon England's elite flyers to help deal with a monster. His colleagues were less composed. They burst out laughing. For a moment, the merry noise echoed off the hallowed walls. The Royal Air Force being called to hunt a monster! It was absurd! Hilarious! Then, another politician spoke over the din. He asked, "Would not the Scottish Office find its time better occupied in trying to capture the monster of unemployment in Scotland?" The laughter fizzled. It was a good question.

Money and jobs were scarce throughout the UK. In 1921, a fourth of Scotland's population was out of work. Over the next decade, that number would creep up until nearly a third of

Scots were unemployed. People were stressed, desperate, and humiliated. Folks who couldn't scrounge up enough work to feed themselves or pay rent turned to the "dole," which was government relief in the form of meager payments that just barely covered the cost of living. Money for the dole came from local taxes, paid by community members who were often barely hanging on themselves. People were hungry. One study found that nearly 40 percent of children in the UK were either undernourished or malnourished.

Just when things seemed like they couldn't get any worse, the American stock markets tanked in 1929, plunging the United States into a financial crisis. Americans yanked their remaining money from overseas holdings, stopped importing products from Europe and elsewhere, and hunkered down. This drove Scotland's economy further into the ground. Many industries dried up. Even people who were lucky enough to hang on to their jobs struggled. An average Scottish industrial worker earned about one shilling an hour in 1933. This meant that it would take him an hour of labor to afford a pound of butter, twenty-one hours of work to buy a new kilt, and fifty-five hours to earn himself a woolen coat. Living through such a hard time taught many Scots to be frugal and always watch for opportunities to make money.

Anger hung like a cloud over impacted nations. Resentment, too. People blamed financial institutions for the disaster. Author John Steinbeck later put his fury about these dark days into words in his novel, *The Grapes of Wrath*: "The bank is something more than men, I tell you. It's the monster. Men made it, but they can't control it." The Loch Ness Monster wasn't anything like Steinbeck's "monster" banks. As the financial institutions sank, they took people's money with them. In contrast, every time the Loch Ness Monster surfaced, it dropped a coin or two into Scottish pockets.

The most obvious way that the Loch Ness Monster boosted the economy was through tourism. People from all over the UK and abroad read stories about the beast and wanted to see it for themselves. This meant they traveled to Loch Ness. They bought tickets for the train or bus. Automobile drivers filled up on fuel at local stations. Attendants at formerly quiet gas stations soon reported servicing up to 1,000 cars a day. Once they arrived, these visitors had more needs, like food, lodging, and entertainment. Highlanders scrambled to accommodate their new guests, converting homes into tea rooms and shrugging apologetically at the bumper-to-bumper traffic. One hotel's logbook showed just how far people had traveled to see the beast. Guests had arrived from "New Zealand, Chicago, Siam [Thailand], the Sudan, Ceylon [Sri Lanka], Johannesburg . . . , Paris, Ireland, Berlin, Gibraltar, the Punjab [India], Italy, Sydney and Melbourne . . . Hong Kong, Hamburg, Canada, Alexandria, south Persia [Iran], Tanganyika [Tanzania], Rangoon [Yangon], Madras [Chennai], Durban, Amsterdam, Vienna, Detroit, and New Jersey."

Men like David MacBrayne were perfectly positioned to profit from Loch Ness Monster mania. He owned a Loch Ness ferry boat called the "Gondolier," onto which he piled eager tourists. MacBrayne ran two cruises a day, taking passengers on a three-hour ride from one end of the loch to another before turning around and doing the trip in reverse. The price for an adult ticket was six shillings. MacBrayne did such a brisk business that he had to add an additional ferry to his fleet to handle the crowds.

Other industrious Scots were quick to whip up souvenirs for visitors to purchase and take home. Monster-themed postcards, trinkets, and jigsaw puzzles flew off the shelves. These became popular even outside of the Highlands. At the British Industries Fair in London, for example, vendors sold delightful little Loch Ness Monster toys. These were so tempting that even the Queen of England couldn't resist picking one up herself. She remarked that the mini monster had her "much amused." The vendor selling the monster toys surely didn't care if the queen thought they were funny or scary. Money was money. Another person who recognized the value of a good laugh was comedian and musician, Tommy Torrance. After realizing

Monster watchers, 1933

how profitable the monster was, he trotted into an Edinburgh recording studio to crank out a catchy song called "I'm looking for the Loch Ness Monster."

Even businesses that had no connection to Loch Ness whatsoever made quick work of latching on to the monster to boost sales. By November 1933, Colman's Mustard was running large advertisements featuring a snakelike lake beast and hawking "monster" tins of its golden mustard. The tagline read, "Can you swallow that?" In December, Chisholm's department store ran ads shouting, "Loch Ness Contains a Monster, but it's nothing to the 'Monster' Display of Xmas Gifts at Chisholm's." Within months, the monster was splashed across advertisements for everything from potted flowers to fish dinners to hazelnut chocolate bars. A leavening agent called Lance's Baking Powder appealed to customer's literary sensibilities with a poem:

> They are wondering whatever this monster can be
> That all the people are flocking to see;
> If only they could make him rise,
> They'd see his shape and see his size;
> And all they need do to be really wise,
> It's ever so simple, so easy to guess,
> Why, just pop some LANCE'S into Loch Ness.

In fact, the monster proved itself to be such a moneymaker that some people outside of Scotland began to feel jealous. In December, a Parisian journalist accused people in the Scottish tourism industry of inventing the monster as a way to grow their businesses. The Austrian government would later express its own irritation, claiming that the monster was part of a scheme to draw tourists away from Austria and into Scotland. This sentiment was echoed by others around the world who saw the moneymaking potential of the mysterious beast.

At first, the sums passed around Loch Ness were relatively small: a few pounds for a hotel room here, a few shillings for a monster knickknack there. Taken on their own, they were insignificant. But added together, they served to prop up whole communities of Highlanders who suddenly had enough cash to buy dinner *and* pay their rent. It was a glorious relief in an otherwise dark and hungry time.

In December 1933, George Spicer made a reappearance. The buttoned-up London tailor who'd shared his account of seeing the Loch Ness Monster cross the road back in July had more to say about the whole thing. He wanted to change a few details, too. Spicer marched into the London BBC Radio studios and gave an interview. He'd originally reported that the monster was four or five feet high and about six to eight feet long, a fairly dainty beast when compared with the accounts that followed. Now, four months and dozens of newspaper reports later, Spicer corrected himself. The beast was *thirty* feet long. Listeners swooned with excitement. The formerly quiet tailor found himself quite enjoying the spotlight. Spicer later bragged "I broadcast to twenty million people" and "have letters from all over the world."

As the Loch Ness monster supposedly grew in size, it grew in value as well thanks to a famous London circus owner named Bertram Mills.

When Mills read newspaper tales of a giant and mysterious beast in Loch Ness, he knew he had to have it for his show. The crowd appeal would be unprecedented! He issued a public call for help which was promptly printed in newspapers in England,

Scotland, Wales, and Ireland. Anyone who could capture the Loch Ness Monster and deliver it to him in London would get a payment of £20,000 ($23,424). His offer wasn't a joke. He issued a set of conditions. The hunter would be paid only if "the monster proves to be at least 20 feet long, weighing not less than 1,000lb, and a creature believed to be extinct. It must not be a whale, large eel shark, nor other fish or animal which is found in these latitudes." Mills wasn't about to shell out all that cash for an oversize catfish. He promised to bring in a crew of experts to verify the particulars once the creature had been nabbed and transported to him. Proving just how serious Mills was about his monster hunt, he took out an insurance policy on his offer through a respected firm called Lloyd's.

Mills didn't appear to be the only one putting a bounty on the monster's head. Stories soon began circulating about Dr. W. Reid Blair, the fifty-nine-year-old director of New York's Bronx Zoo, who announced that he'd pay $25,000 for the monster. Like Mills, he listed a few conditions. It had to be forty feet long, and "in good health." Dr. Blair added, "I don't want any sick monster on my hands." Unlike Mills's offer, Blair's offer wasn't serious. He'd said it as a joke. Newspaper reporters who were either caught up in the excitement of the moment or unconcerned about facts ignored this. They printed Blair's reward as though it were legitimate.

These stories made the Loch Ness Monster's existence seem more probable. If successful businessman and scientists were willing to invest real money, then the monster had to be real. Plus, it wasn't that out of left field to imagine that a strange and terrifying creature could be discovered right under people's noses. This sort of thing actually happened pretty regularly in the 1930s.

CHAPTER 8

SCIENCE

"All about us there is something new to discover. He who is alert may discover something every day of his life. The age of discovery is bequeathed to us all!"

— George Matthew Adams, newspaper columnist, 1934

he 1930s were an age in which scientific discoveries came so hot and fast that it was almost impossible to stay on top of them. Zoology, especially, experienced explosive growth. In the years leading up to Loch Ness Monster mania, Western scientists identified around 12,000 new species each year. That means that an average of thirty-three living things were given scientific names each day.

In 1910, one of these discoveries sent shock waves around the world. That year, a Dutch civil administrator named First Lieutenant J. K. H. van Steyn van Hensbroek was stationed in a Dutch colony on a small Indonesian island. He began hearing rumors that nearby Komodo Island was crawling with awful, dragon-like beasts. These buaya darat, or "land crocodiles," were big enough to take down huge water buffalo. They had sharp teeth, daggerlike claws, and powerful bodies. Though van Hensbroek wasn't the first Westerner to hear these stories, he appears to have been the first to take them seriously. He set out to Komodo Island in question, eager to see the buaya darat himself. It wasn't long before the young lieutenant experienced the shock of a lifetime. Komodo Island really was crawling with dragons. Komodo dragons are every inch the fearsome monster van Hensbroek had been told they were. They're the biggest living reptiles on the planet, reaching up to ten feet in length and three hundred pounds. When pursuing prey, they can dart at speeds of up to 12 miles per hour. On top of everything else, their saliva is toxic. A single bite can be deadly. Van Hensbroek made quick work of killing one of the beasts and sending it to a Dutch scientist to study. The scientist was similarly floored. *Dragons were real.*

When word of Komodo dragons spread among Western populations, it seemed as though medieval tales had come to life. Newspaper stories thrilled readers with descriptions of these giant, scaly, deadly beasts that might as well have marched straight out of King Arthur's court. They even slept in deep burrows, just like the dragons in fairy tales who slept in caves or lairs. Learning about Komodo dragons was a shock. It also begged the question: if dragons walked the earth, what other mythical creatures might turn out to be real?

The answer came from the sea: the Kraken. This mythical water monster was born of Scandinavian mythology and famed for dragging ships under the sea in violent, terrifying attacks. The Kraken was said to be huge, with long, tentacled arms and a voracious appetite. It swam in such powerful circles that it formed deadly whirlpools in the sea. What's more, it appeared to delight in swallowing sailors whole. Just before Loch Ness Monster fever hit the world, the Kraken, like the Komodo dragon, jumped off storybook pages and into the news.

In 1925, a group of Antarctic sailors sliced into a sperm whale's belly. Inside, they found a pair of enormous tentacles lined with rows of razor-sharp claws and circular suckers ringed with serrated teeth. Had they recovered evidence of the Kraken? They gathered the pulpy tentacles and sent them off to a British scientist. His careful study of the rotting, ropy appendages revealed that the sailors had not actually found a mythical beast, but instead had discovered something more exciting: the remains of a new species called the colossal squid.

Over the following years, as more body parts turned up from these elusive creatures, scientists realized that colossal squid were nearly as monstrous as the mythical Kraken. From the top of their mantles to tip of their tentacles, colossal squid can grow to an incredible forty-five feet. Their giant, unblinking eyes are the size of soccer balls. Found only in the very deep, cold waters off Antarctica, their discovery reinforced the fact that the earth still held countless mysteries for scientists to uncover.

On January 14, 1933, just months before the excitement began at Loch Ness, a group of pedestrians on a beach in Scarborough, a seaside town in North Yorkshire, England, uncovered a mystery of their own. Something terrible lay on the sand. Its slick skin was blotchy and mottled. Long, snaky ropes trailed limply from its body. People crowded around, wondering what it was. A local naturalist heard news of the commotion and hustled to the waterfront to behold their treasure. He marveled at the sight. It was, he decided, the largest cephalopod ever to have washed ashore in England: a giant squid.

Giant squid had been seen plenty of times before, but never so close to British shores. Normally, these massive creatures were confined to black ocean depths off the American East Coast, or off the southern tip of Africa. This mammoth corpse showed that they were closer to England than anyone had thought. Stories about their ferocity were trickling back to England, too. Only recently, a Royal Norwegian Navy ship called the *Brunswick* had experienced multiple attacks from a furious giant squid. The slimy monster hadn't had any luck, of course. It didn't stand a chance in bringing down a fifteen-thousand-ton tanker. But the squid's fierce attacks were a reminder nonetheless: some of the sea's inhabitants were distinctly unfriendly.

The mysteries of the deep were terrifying to some and alluring to others. For British naturalist William Beebe and engineer Otis Barton, they were an irresistible temptation. Between 1930 and 1934, the pair made thirty-five deep-sea dives inside a laughably tiny submarine that Barton had built himself. The duo climbed inside the five-foot-wide spherical chamber, knees knocking together, and descended to depths that would exceed three thousand feet—a record. Through three tiny windows, they peered into a dark and alien world. "In these strange, somber depths swim monsters stranger than their surroundings," one science journalist noted, "monsters so weird and bizarre that they resemble creatures out of a nightmare." Beebe and Barton's trips under the sea captivated armchair scientists everywhere. Their exploits were so daring, so exciting, that they were reported in newspapers around the world. One of their dives was even broadcast live over the radio for audiences in North America and Europe. People couldn't get enough of their nightmare creatures.

The majority of zoological advances occurred with far less fanfare. Scientists tromped through thick brush holding butterfly nets or peered at swimming blobs under microscope lenses. They published academic papers and gave creatures long, impossible-to-pronounce Latin names. The sheer number of living things on the planet gave these scholars the ultimate sense of job security. They would never run out of work on a planet so buzzing with life.

While zoologists were busy cataloging all of their new discoveries, paleontologists in the 1930s were up to their elbows in piles of newly uncovered fossilized bones. There were Niger's T. rex-like beast called the *Carcharodontosaurus*, complete with a mouthful of steak-knife teeth and spindly forearms, and Egypt's colossal sauropod, *Aegyptosaurus*. These creatures reminded people that the Earth had long been teeming with strange, fantastic, and often monstrous life-forms. London's *Daily Mail* seized upon this fact, running a multipart series called "These Monsters DID Live." Each day, a different dinosaur drawing appeared alongside Loch Ness Monster coverage.

This cascade of scientific discovery helped elevate the Loch Ness Monster from an improbable

THESE MONSTERS DID LIVE! (No. 7)

Pelycosaurian, one of a division of saurian reptiles belonging to the carboniferous or permocarboniferous epoch. Its length was about 8ft.

Daily Mail, January 6, 1934

myth into something that might actually be real. The Loch Ness Monster was no less believable than a bunch of lethal dragons running amok in Indonesia, or a giant, angry beast attacking Norwegian naval ships. The sheer number of Loch Ness Monster eyewitness accounts certainly suggested that some yet-unknown creature was in the loch.

To determine what exactly the monster was, scientists needed evidence. A live specimen would have been ideal. A dead monster would also work. Scientists needed a body to poke, prod, dissect, and measure. They wanted to peer into the beast's open jaw, to examine its diet, to peel back its skin, and to weigh its bones. Even this became news. The *Daily Mail* devoted two-thirds of a page to a story about how intensely scientists craved evidence of the monster: "So keen is the modern zoologist on his job that he would sell his soul for the dead carcass of a dinosaur or plesiosaur so that he might be the first to have the honor of dissecting it," an anthropologist told the *Mail*. He lamented the lack of physical proof for "monstrosaurus," as he called the Loch Ness Monster, moaning that they had "not even a scale or a hair of his skin or a nail of a toe."

While they waited for a body, scientists, newspapermen, and the general public had to content themselves with the only evidence available: photographs.

CHAPTER 9

PICTURES

"You expect to photograph it?"
"If it's there, you bet I'll photograph it."
"Suppose it doesn't like having its
picture taken?"   —*King Kong*, 1933

Photography in the 1930s was entirely unlike photography today. Cameras back then were expensive, finicky contraptions made of polished wood, leather, and glass. They had accordions to release, snaps to loosen, and lenses to uncover. Film was either spooled onto bulky canisters, which had to then be artfully threaded into the camera, or fused onto rectangles of fragile glass. Whatever type of film a person used, they had to keep it carefully covered until they were ready to take their picture. Otherwise, it would be ruined. Once the camera was loaded and ready, it had to be perfectly positioned and focused on its subject. This in itself was tricky, as the viewfinders were often very basic. If the lighting was dim, a long exposure might be required. This meant that the camera needed to be very still for several seconds while the image was captured. Bulky wooden tripods helped ensure that a photograph wouldn't be blurry, but took additional time to set up. In short, capturing photos in the 1930s could be a real pain in the neck.

Despite all the trouble it caused, photography was still a crucial way to communicate information, especially for something new or unknown. When Amelia Earhart became the first woman to fly solo across the Atlantic in 1932, newspaper editors clamored for images of the "aviatrix" and her plane. It was as if the world needed to see images of the female pilot to believe she existed at all. Similarly, many wanted to see photographs of the Loch Ness Monster—something almost as unbelievable as a woman aviator.

In order to answer this need, photographers began trickling into the Highlands. First came ex-army officer, Captain Ellisford, "a well-known amateur photographer." Ellisford was ready for anything. He arrived on the loch lugging a "large box of modern photographic material," including a "telephoto lens." Unfortunately, Ellisford did all that packing for nothing. His efforts were unrewarded. Hoping someone else might have better luck, the *News Chronicle* put out an enticing offer: £100 ($117) for a photograph of the Loch Ness Monster. Of course, the paper wouldn't accept any old image. It required that the image be "vouched for by three responsible persons." Like Ellisford, the *Chronicle* came up empty-handed.

Other newspapers took things up a notch. They began sending correspondents to the Highlands in the hopes that they might interview witnesses, find evidence of the monster's existence, or—even better—see it themselves. The *Scotsman* was the first to put one of its writers on an official monster watch in late October, but the *Daily Express* was hot on its heels. It sent its own reporter to Loch Ness shortly after. Before long, one Highlander would note that newspapermen were suddenly "falling all over one another in their daily patrol of Loch Ness." The air hummed with giddy anticipation: *what would happen next?*

In November 1933, that question was answered when a celebrity named Lieutenant Commander Rupert Gould arrived in Loch Ness. Every inch of Gould's six-foot, four-inch frame oozed charisma. He had a handsome, winning smile, and he wore his mop of brown hair in a loose pompadour. In addition to being a well-known BBC Radio personality, he was a noted expert on a wide range of bizarre topics. Over the course of his career, he authored books covering everything from *Oddities* to *Enigmas*. With this career trajectory, it made perfect sense that he'd wind up at Loch Ness. After all, what was odder or more enigmatic than a Scottish sea serpent?

Gould came to Loch Ness with a clear agenda. He wanted to investigate monster sightings and provide his expert analysis. He also likely saw a chance to market and sell his latest book, *The Case for the Sea Serpent*. Upon arriving in the Highlands, Gould purchased a tiny secondhand motorcycle which he named Cynthia, and set off on a tour of the loch's rocky shoreline. The broad-shouldered academic spent two weeks puttering around the loch on his petite steed and interviewing more than fifty eyewitnesses. Newspapers reported on Gould's progress, as well as his credentials. They described him as a "high naval officer" and a "recognized authority upon marine monsters." This made Gould's investigation seem terribly official and important.

As excitement surrounding Gould's expedition rippled outward from Scotland, a new piece of monster evidence made a splash of its own. On December 6, newspapers printed a blurry, confusing photograph that appeared to show an object floating on dark water. The accompanying story was just as hard to understand as the image itself.

A British Aluminum company employee named Hugh Gray claimed he had taken the photo weeks earlier while walking home from church. Mid-stroll, he decided to rest along the loch's edge. "I had hardly sat down on the bank when an object of considerable dimensions rose out of the loch two hundred yards away," he later told a journalist. "I immediately got my camera into position and snapped the object which was two or three feet above the surface of the water." This was an impressive feat, given the complicated nature of 1930s photography. Gray then completed his walk home, put the film into a drawer, and, strangely, did absolutely nothing with it. The undeveloped film—which promised to show the world's most popular and mysterious monster—lingered there until Gray's brother discovered it and had it developed. When the photograph was printed, Gray acted surprised. He said, "I understand that a good picture of the monster, or whatever the object is, was seen." He then tried to explain his delay in sharing the image, noting that he didn't want anyone to make fun of him for believing in the monster. "I was afraid of the chaff which the workmen and others would shower upon me," he said.

Perhaps in acknowledgment of Gray's odd behavior, or of the image's poor quality, several newspapers printed it alongside a note that the negative had been examined by representatives of the Eastman Kodak Company. These professionals determined that the film had not been edited or otherwise tampered with. Gray further validated the whole thing by standing before a magistrate and swearing that he was telling the truth.

A group of zoologists at Glasgow University was quick to

analyze Gray's photograph. They issued a disappointing verdict. Professor Graham Kerr complained that the image didn't even appear to show a living creature at all. He called the photo "utterly unconvincing." Largely ignoring this disappointing analysis, the press continued to share Gray's story and image. One paper even nicknamed Gray "The Man Who Snapped the Monster." In addition to newspaper coverage, Gray also broadcast his fascinating tale to all of Scotland over the radio.

Days after Gray's photo bombshell, Gould reentered the fray. He wrote up his official conclusion about the happenings at Loch Ness and tried to sell it to the Press Association, a British

Hugh Gray's "monster" photograph

news agency. Surprisingly, they wouldn't take the piece. While so many competitive news organizations were printing all sorts of unverified monster fluff, the Press Association showed unique restraint. "We don't want that," a representative told Gould, "We don't believe in it." An annoyed Gould looked elsewhere. On December 9, the London *Times* shared his speculative verdict: "Loch Ness contains at least one specimen of the rarest and least known of all living creatures."

At the same time that Gould and Gray were filling columns of newsprint with questionable monster content, a company called Scottish Film Productions headed to the loch on a fact-finding mission of its own. It stationed a small team of cameramen around the water armed with both still cameras and film cameras. Much as Marmaduke Wetherell's crew had walked through the African bush, waiting to film an elusive lion, these men dug in along a chilly Scottish loch and waited to film a monster. On December 12, the same day that Parliament discussed whether the air force might be called in to protect the Loch Ness Monster, Scottish Film Productions struck gold. A crew member named Malcolm Irvine had been on a hillside facing the ruins of Urquhart Castle when a commotion arose in the water about a hundred yards away that caught his attention. Heart pounding, he fumbled for the nearest camera—a moving film camera with a three-inch zoom lens—and hoisted it to his eye. He captured the source of the activity through his view-finder. It was a long, dark object that seemed to be moving across the surface of the loch. He later estimated that it traveled at about nine to ten miles per hour, and noted that it left a "trail of foam" in its wake. The footage is less than one minute long, though Irvine later recalled that it "seemed like hours" when he was filming it. Then, the creature submerged, leaving Irvine reeling. He could hardly believe it. He'd filmed the beast!

Much like Hugh Gray's monster photo, Irvine's monster film is hard to interpret. He correctly noted that he'd captured *something* on the water, but what it is cannot be determined. One journalist quickly dismissed the film, reporting that its starring creature was "certainly a seal." Others were happy to believe that Irvine had filmed the monster. Editors at the *Hartlepool Northern Daily Mail* clearly believed the footage was genuine. That paper proclaimed that the film didn't just show a monster. It also showed its humps, fins, and tail.

In mid-December 1933, a German newspaper called *Deutsche Allgemeine Zeitung* added to the tangle of monster news. It reported that retired U-boat commander Georg-Günther Freiherr von Forstner had seen something very similar to the Loch Ness Monster off the coast of France. He claimed that his sighting, which he had not mentioned publicly before, had occurred in a moment of chaos back in 1915 during World War I. Von Forstner's submarine had just torpedoed a British steamer called the *Iberian*. As the British ship sank under the sea, her boilers exploded. This sent pieces of wreckage rocketing upward. Von Forstner and five crew members watched the mayhem, probably quite enjoying their wartime victory. But then, in the middle of the flotsam, he said a "gigantic sea monster was hurled, writhing and struggling, twenty or thirty yards into the air." Von Forstner said he'd stood there, gaping, while a sixty-foot-long monster soared overhead. It had four webbed limbs, a tapered head, and a long tail, much like an enormous flying crocodile. It splashed down and disappeared into the depths, leaving behind the baffled Germans. Von Forstner's story was questionable, yet thrilling.

It ran in newspapers from London, England to Muncie, Indiana to Montreal, Canada.

Fervent monster believers reveled in the daily news. There were just so many sightings, so many tales. It seemed like hardly a day could pass without new monster reports. *Surely*, they shrugged, *so many people couldn't be wrong*. This line of reasoning irritated some scientists who knew that large groups of people could, of course, be mistaken. E. G. Boulenger, the aquarium director at the London Zoo said, "The case of the Monster in Loch Ness is worthy of our consideration if only because it presents a striking example of mass hallucination." Another expert agreed. Anthropologist Sir Arthur Keith wrote to the *Daily Mail*, explaining that "the existence or nonexistence of the 'monster' is not a problem for zoologists but for psychologists."

Boulenger, Keith, and others like them, wouldn't be satisfied until the beast had been dragged onto the rocky shoreline for thorough examination. They wanted a body. And for that, they needed a hunter.

CHAPTER 10

MARMADUKE

And so, at the end of 1933, London's *Daily Mail* approached Marmaduke Wetherell, the big-game hunter and filmmaker from the beginning of this book, with an unusual question: fancy a monster hunt?

The *Mail* had spent the 1920s as England's top newspaper. Back then it had a circulation, or readership, that topped out at about 1.8 million. This meant that a quarter of the daily newspapers sold in England had the *Daily Mail*'s elaborate masthead embossed across the top. Publishers there achieved this success by understanding what kind of news typical readers wanted, and how they wanted to get it. Earlier newspaper powerhouses had filled their pages with long columns of dreadfully serious, boring, and confusing accounts of politics or finance. These newspapers catered to an elite, educated crowd. The *Daily Mail* turned this convention on its head. It began churning out papers aimed at a much wider audience with a much shorter attention span. It printed brief, splashy stories alongside eye-catching graphics. It focused on high-interest topics, such as social scandals, the royal family, and crime. Ironically, the "busy man's paper" also featured a page just for women, which printed stories on "dress, toilette matters, cookery, and home matters." The *Mail* additionally kept readers hooked by staging various "stunts." These were paper-sponsored expeditions, challenges, and contests designed to drum up interest and sell papers. Some stunts were successful, such as the 1906 aviation challenge to fly from London to Manchester for a £10,000 ($11,712) prize. Others were a flop, such as the 1920 "Hat Campaign," in which fashion-forward subscribers were asked to design the hat of the future for a £1,000 ($1,171) prize. The winner was a disappointing top hat and bowler mash-up that never caught on. Taken together, the stunts, quick and entertaining stories, women's page, and social gossip made the *Mail* into a news giant.

Publishers at rival papers saw the *Mail*'s success and followed suit. They also began cranking out short, simple articles and just-for-women content. Editors pushed stories that were wilder, more extreme, and more entertaining than ever before. When news events occurred, newspaper editors scrambled to out-scoop one another. Reporters darted onto accident scenes to snag quotes from witnesses. Telegraph cables whizzed across oceans and continents. This battle for readers was part of a period known as the newspaper wars, and it often pushed reporters to extremes to produce the punchiest story of the day. This wasn't anything new. In the late 19th century, two New York newspapers had gotten so wrapped up in their own battle for readers that a new term was coined to describe their senstational, exaggerated, problematic copy: yellow journalism. Around the same time, the *Daily Mail* stretched its own standards, occasionally featuring completely made-up content. For example, the *Mail* ran a series of love letters that appeared to be from heartsick readers, but which were actually dreamed up by in-house writers. One, between two anonymous lovers who went by "Oak" and "Ivy," was especially dramatic. In one letter, Oak told Ivy he was leaving her to travel to Africa. Ivy couldn't let her beau go. She followed up with a letter of her own: "If you go to Africa, I shall follow." This scandalous back-and-forth kept readers glued to their papers and buying new copies each day to see what would happen next. Tactics like fabricated drama, contests, and stunts made newspapers into entertaining products that mixed fact and fiction without clearly identifying either.

When the *Daily Mail* invited Wetherell on its monster hunt, the paper was simply staging its next battle in this ongoing newspaper war. Editors at the *Mail* needed this monster hunt stunt to be a success. In 1931, just before Loch Ness Monster mania struck the world, the *Daily Mail* had suddenly dropped from first place to third in circulation numbers. This was a monumental shift in newspaper standings. It also made the paper's invitation to Wetherell terribly important. The *Mail* needed a splashy story. Could Wetherell deliver it?

It had been a very busy year for the actor-turned-hunter-turned director. He had released three films, including *Wanderlust*, and looked forward to beginning his next giant project, a film called *The Silent Rancher*. He had also established himself as a keen and creative advertiser who manipulated the press to his advantage. In the fall of 1933, he ran a newspaper "actress wanted" ad that included the following requirements:

> Young, pretty, blonde, with a complexion able to stand
> the daylight without makeup, able to act on the stage or
> for the screen and change parts nightly, prepared to travel
> 20,000 miles partly through the jungle, able to make a

ballroom scene at a Red Sea temperature of 100 in the shade, indifferent to mosquitos, snakes, crocodiles and lions except when the plot demands attention to such details.

The job listing was so outlandish that it became a news item in itself. People wondered what kind of movie might be forthcoming, and pondered the man behind the ad. It was a brilliant example of early viral marketing.

The *Daily Mail*'s monster hunt invitation was another unconventional advertising opportunity for Wetherell. By taking on the project, he would be guaranteed space in one of Britain's top newspapers. Though the *Daily Mail*'s coverage would focus on his quest to find the Loch Ness Monster, it would undoubtedly also mention his films, one of which was in theaters that very month. By participating in the *Mail*'s monster hunt, Wetherell might even manage to one-up his "actress wanted" viral marketing moment.

It was the perfect time for Wetherell to step into the spotlight. He had spent the previous decade inching upward, both in the cinematic world, and in London's most educated circles. His work on *Livingstone* hadn't earned him much box office success, but it had gotten his name on the lips of the right people. Two months after its release, he was nominated to become a Fellow of the Royal Geographical Society. This group had a storied history and a roster of well-known explorers. Men like Charles Darwin and David Livingstone had been fellows. There were a handful of celebrity fellows as well, including Robert Ripley, of Ripley's *Believe it or Not*. Joining this group allowed Wethrell to add some impressive letters after his name: FRGS.

In 1926, Wetherell added even more letters after his name

by becoming a fellow of the Zoological Society of London (FZS). This was yet another respected organization, once thought of as one of the "most influential and learned societies of England." Zoological Society of London fellows were among the naturalists who spent their careers adding to the ever-growing list of newly identified species. They gave impressive names to snails, worms, ducks, and more. When they weren't out identifying new species, they spent their time inside the London Zoological Gardens, the world's first scientific zoo. They also published papers with laborious titles like, "Notes on the Breeding of Several Birds in the Society's Gardens During the Year 1867."

In addition to his professional growth, Wetherell's reputation had grown as well. His outsize personality made him a standout in social circles. Some people loved him. They described him as "funny" and "intelligent." Others found him hard to tolerate. Peter Fleming, a BBC Radio producer (and brother of Ian Fleming, creator of James Bond), disliked Wetherell. He described him as "dense."

The *Daily Mail*'s monster hunt invitation would have placed Wetherell at a tricky crossroads. Participating in a fruitless search could ruin his reputation. Or it might just elevate him to a new level of fame. He had managed to achieve moderate success with his films and had been accepted into important social circles. Would agreeing put all of his hard work at risk?

On December 14, news spread that two screenwriters were preparing to make a Loch Ness Monster film. Tentatively titled *Sinister Deeps*, the movie would tell the story of how villagers around a small Scottish loch dealt with a fearsome water beast. It was a great, timely idea for a blockbuster film. The screenwriters already had a production company secured. They were set to begin filming the next month. As Wetherell contemplated his next steps, the screenwriters arrived at Loch Ness to scout locations and talent.

Also in December 1933, RKO Pictures released a sequel to *King Kong* called *Son of Kong*. In it, a long-necked water dinosaur makes several menacing appearances to terrify the unfortunate passengers of a dinghy. *Son of Kong* had been thrown together in just nine months. Such a speedy production required some creative thinking on the part of the filmmakers, including reusing the first movie's famed brontosaurus model. For *Son of Kong*, the special effects team modified the dinosaur only slightly, adding a bumpy texture to its neck. This made it reminiscent of Commander Meiklem's monster sighting, which he'd claimed had been "dotted with knobbly lumps." Movies were clearly reflecting the hubbub around Loch Ness. Wetherell was a seasoned moviemaker. If he wanted to jump on this monster bandwagon, he needed to do it soon. He was in real danger of being eclipsed by another adventure hunter with a camera. The pressure was on.

Wetherell made his decision the next day. He would hunt the monster.

Almost immediately, Wetherell made it clear that he understood what the *Daily Mail* needed from him. Sure, he'd been hired to find a monster. But more than that, he'd been hired to stage a drama for *Mail* readers. He needed to tell a captivating story. He got right to work, approaching the monster hunt the way he'd approached so many of his films. First, he cast a co-star by inviting an old film buddy named Gustav Pauli to join him on the hunt. An experienced cameraman as well as a distinguished-looking fellow, Pauli added credibility and class to the endeavor. He also made the perfect sidekick.

The two moviemakers arrived at Loch Ness on December 18.

That evening, Wetherell met with a reporter from the *Inverness Courier*. Wetherell played his part perfectly. He smiled at the Scottish journalist, then said ominously, "the loch is the most eerie place I have ever been round, especially with the mist and heavy clouds overhanging the mountains." One could almost hear the movie soundtrack in the background.

Wetherell then set the scene. He said that he felt hesitant about his ability to find the monster. He was intimidated and overwhelmed. "After seeing the huge loch itself," he confessed, "I cannot conceive a more difficult task than trying to photograph the "monster." He continued, "Other than with phenomenal luck, there is very little chance of photographing it." Wetherell laid out the stakes for his audience as though he were the protagonist in an action film. His needed to find the beast. But there were obstacles in his way that he'd somehow have to overcome. The loch was huge. The monster, reclusive. "By the time that Mr. Pauli had got his lens in position, the 'monster' might be in some other place, or perhaps have completely disappeared," he cautioned. This primed the audience. It set their expectations low and reminded them of just how daunting this task would be. As if to emphasize Wetherell's point, the loch churned angrily. Wind tore across its surface, whipping it into foamy whitecaps.

At the same time that Wetherell was preparing his audience, a group of workers across the loch was transforming a farm field into an airstrip. They yanked fence posts and beams free of the earth until they'd cleared enough space for two small aircraft to land. A local airline pilot, Captain Fresson, wanted to embark upon an aerial monster hunt of his own. He planned to search the loch from above, flying low and slow over the water and peering into its depths.

Wetherell's carefully crafted plot suddenly thickened. He had competition. This meant that if he wanted to give the *Daily Mail* its monster, he needed to get to work. Fast.

Captain E.E. Fresson (far right) prepares for his aerial search for the monster.

CHAPTER 11

THE HUNT

Marmaduke Wetherell had faced many grueling challenges over the course of his career. He'd filmed wild animals and fussy actors, and sweated in tropical heat. Once, he'd gripped the edges of his canoe as an angry hippo repeatedly tried to knock him into the water. In December 1933, he found himself in a new type of challenging situation: Wetherell needed to find the *Daily Mail* a lake monster while the whole world watched.

Not wanting their readers to miss a single moment of Wetherell's hunt, the *Daily Mail* sent a correspondent named F. W. Memory to Loch Ness. Memory wasn't an expert on monsters or hunting. Rather, he was a seasoned crime reporter who specialized in stories about murder and sudden death. Memory was an important figure at the *Daily Mail*. At the time, crime was one of the most popular topics for newspaper readers. When editors at the *Daily Mail* pulled him away from his normal assignments and sent him to Loch Ness, it showed how seriously the paper took this monster hunt stunt. It also reflected Memory's writing skills. His editors knew he would spin whatever happened into an incredible, nail-biting yarn.

On December 19, Memory followed along as Wetherell and Pauli began their monster hunt in earnest. Both men were dressed for adventure, with Wetherell bundled up in a wrinkled overcoat and floppy hat. Pauli looked like a sporting gentleman in his short breeches, tall socks, and crisp trench coat. A photographer on the scene captured their every heroic move. The pair climbed aboard a small wooden boat. *Click*. Men on shore passed them their supplies. *Click*. Pauli looked excited. Wetherell looked tired. Finally, the pair shoved off, their little boat gliding bravely into the center of the deep, dark lake. *Click*.

Out on the loch, nothing much happened. Wetherell smoked cigarettes and stared out at the water. Pauli fiddled with his camera. Tension mounted. Local monster hunters wouldn't have been terribly surprised that Wetherell's little entourage hadn't seen anything yet. After all, these people had had their

Wetherell and Pauli embark on their monster hunt.

eyes glued to the loch's dark waters for half a year and only some of them had managed to spot the beast. It wasn't as though you could simply conjure the monster out of thin air or will it to appear through sheer determination. The monster had to *want* to surface and you had to be in the right place at the right time to see it. It was a matter of odds. Wetherell shouldn't expect to see the monster right away. To have any real chance of spotting the beast, he and his crew would need to spend weeks or even months at the loch.

While logical, this concept would have been unpleasant for newspaper readers, who had short attention spans and an eager appetite for excitement. Thanks to the *Daily Mail*'s revolutionary formatting, they had grown used to brief, splashy, attention-grabbing stories. They wanted a monster, and the *Mail* had been teasing out its stunt hunt for days already. The clock was ticking.

Then, suddenly, shockingly, Wetherell struck gold.

On December 20, a single day after the *Daily Mail*'s monster hunt had officially begun, newsies standing on street corners had something thrilling to offer their customers. *Monster footprints found! Read all about it!*

Eager monster fans forked over their pennies and flipped to page nine. There, under a screaming headline which took up inches of space and used four different sizes of text, was Memory's declaration: "What is believed to be definite evidence pointing to the existence of an amphibious monster in Loch Ness . . . has been discovered to-day by Mr. M. A. Wetherell." The article laid out out the jaw-dropping details. Wetherell had found a set of large, four-fingered footprints on the loch's shore. He deduced that they'd come from a "very powerful soft-footed animal about 20ft long." The article included Wetherell's speculation that the monster "can breathe like a hippopotamus or crocodile with a nostril out of the water, and, although it may be as big as a house no one might see it." Memory quoted Wetherell as though he were an authority on aquatic monsters. Wetherell played up his expertise as well, noting that he'd found the tracks exactly "where [he] expected."

Readers swooned. Now *this* was a story!

Immediately, rival papers began scrambling to get the tale out to their own readers who had to know—was it true? Many simply regurgitated the *Daily Mail* story, while others managed to snag new, unique details. Some of these early articles about Wetherell's discovery used cautious language. They reported that the hunter "believed" he'd seen evidence, or that he'd "claimed" to have found footprints. These words sent a message to readers to be skeptical. However, other articles reported the event as though Wetherell's claims were absolutely reliable. Several papers printed Wetherell's declaration, "I definitely pledge my reputation" on the existence of "an amphibian in Loch Ness." This, along with the sheer number of articles about Wetherell's footprints, contributed to an environment in which readers weren't sure what to believe.

As though aware that some readers might want more proof that he was telling the truth, Wetherell returned to the footprints the following day for a staged photo op. While there, he posed himself half lying above one of the footprints, holding a ruler in one hand and a set of calipers in another. A cigarette dangled casually from his lips. His rumpled hat sat pushed back on his head. Wetherell was the spitting image of a seasoned explorer in the wild. *Click.*

On December 21, typesetters at the *Daily Mail* splashed an

Wetherell poses with monster tracks.

eye-catching headline across nearly the entire width of their paper: "MONSTER OF LOCH NESS IS NOT LEGEND BUT A FACT." Beneath this gigantic declaration were two huge photographs of Wetherell's team on the hunt. This was unusual. At the time, many newspapers stuck to their regular column format, even when delivering big news. Stretching Wetherell's story across the page practically shouted: *read me!* Monster fans willingly complied. They devoured the story and marveled at its details. What luck Wetherell had enjoyed! What an excellent hunter he must be!

A small group of readers, on the other hand, likely regarded the *Daily Mail*'s story with a bit of skepticism. People familiar with Loch Ness knew that the shoreline was almost entirely covered in rocks and pebbles and would not easily show footprints. If Wetherell's story was true, it meant that his beast must have hopped from the rocks onto a rare spot of soil in order to leave firm, clear prints for later analysis. It was possible, of course, but it was also quite the stroke of luck. In another lucky coincidence, Wetherell had happened to arrive in Scotland with all the supplies necessary to make plaster casts of such footprints. He made a cast of one of the monster's prints, then wrapped it carefully and sent it off to London's British Museum (Natural History). There, he boasted to the press, the experts could study his groundbreaking discovery.

At this point, Wetherell was a beacon of success. He'd delivered exactly what the *Mail* wanted, and his name appeared in dozens of other newspapers across the planet. These same papers soon informed their readers of Wetherell's plans to travel back to London to discuss his findings with the curator of the Zoological Society of London. This, along with his decision to send the footprint casts off to the British Museum, made the *Mail*'s hunt seem perfectly legitimate. Not only had Wetherell found something spectacular, but he'd collected proper evidence and was now consulting with the finest minds in the world.

One of those minds belonged to the Keeper of Zoology at the British Museum, Dr. W. T. Calman. He was a white-haired, bespectacled Scottish Highlander who had devoted his life to studying an underappreciated type of water beast: shellfish. Calman, a forever "student of pond life" was a world-renowned expert on all sorts of shelled and articulated critters. His experience in dealing with yet-unnamed animals, along with his Scottish heritage, made him the perfect person to analyze Wetherell's plaster casts of the monster's footprints. The package arrived on his London desk on December 23. Calman immediately got to work examining its contents. His first reaction seemed promising. The *Daily Mail* wasted no time in printing his opinion: "The cast does not represent the track of any known fossil reptile such as the dinosaur, neither is it the impression of any known aquatic mammal in the British Isles or the rest of the world."

If the world's "pond life" expert hadn't been able to instantly identify the tracks, did that mean that Wetherell had, indeed, found evidence of the monster? It certainly appeared possible. Excitement was at a fever pitch. BBC Radio invited Wetherell to treat their listeners to a talk about his exciting discovery on Christmas Eve in their nationwide broadcast.

The only thing more thrilling than Scotland's lake monster was the arrival of Father Christmas. For a few days at the end of December 1933, the Loch Ness Monster faded from the news. Businesses and museums closed, as did scientific institutions. Calman set Wetherell's plaster cast down and headed home to enjoy a Christmas pudding. He would resume his examination in the New Year.

Though the economic crisis continued to darken much of the UK and elsewhere, the small towns around Loch Ness were brightly lit that holiday season. For the first time ever, the loch side city of Inverness glowed with electric lamps. Adding to the festive atmosphere, colored Christmas lights twinkled from the city's railway station and chief public buildings. Monster mania had transformed the area into a magical, charmed place. More and more people were claiming to have seen the beast, including a gentleman who had spotted an impressive "eight or nine humps" on the creature's back. Speculation became a new hobby, with locals suggesting that the monster was everything from a tortoise to a diplodocus to an escaped pet crocodile. Wetherell even chimed in with an unusual animal comparison. He said the footprints "were very much like those of the hippo." No one knew it at the time, but Wetherell had just shown his hand.

Rather than latch onto Wetherell's suggestion, Highlanders mostly ignored it. They were too busy celebrating the season and their new, delightful monster. In Inverness, people raised their glasses to a successful New Year, toasting "Here's to the monster. May his shadows never grow less."

The days ticked by, folding 1933 into 1934. Still the world waited for the British Museum's official verdict on Wetherell's monster footprints. Perhaps sensing that his fame was in danger of fading, Wetherell took out a giant banner ad in the *Era* on January 3. It proclaimed, "NEW YEAR WISHES TO ALL FRIENDS IN THE TRADE FROM M. A. WETHERELL, LOCH NESS." The ad served only two purposes: to keep the name Wetherell fresh in people's minds, and to make sure that it was linked with Loch Ness. Wetherell needn't have worried. His name would soon become permanently associated with the Loch Ness Monster. He wouldn't just be famous. He'd be infamous.

One day after Wetherell's New Year's ad, the *Daily Mail* printed a disappointing letter from Dr. W. T. Calman. The zoologist's initial finding that the cast hadn't come from any known marine mammal needed to be updated. After careful study, Calman had changed his mind. He determined that the footprints were actually from a very well-known creature that had no business tromping around a Scottish loch. They had come, from of all things, a *hippopotamus*. This was a creature not native to Scotland but to Africa, a continent on which one particular hunter had spent plenty of time. "We are unable to find any significant difference between these impressions and the foot of a hippopotamus," the letter stated. Then things got even weirder. Calman went on to declare that the prints had all come from the same limb, the right rear foot of a taxidermied female hippopotamus.

The news surely struck a blow to the folks at the *Daily Mail*, who had been telling their readers for weeks about their trustworthy, intrepid, skillful hunter who would put an end to this mystery once and for all. The paper had printed news of his footprint discovery as though it was a legitimate scientific breakthrough. Now, the editors faced a serious problem. Instead of ensuring that readers understood their error, they buried Calman's verdict in an article under the misleading headline "MONSTER MYSTERY DEEPENS." A more accurate title would have been "LOCH NESS TRACKS CAME FROM HIPPO." The *Mail* made a quick acknowledgment of Calman's findings but didn't linger on them or label Wetherell's deceit. It sailed right past these dull details and instead focused on the exciting possibility that the monster might have been feasting on local deer.

For his part, Wetherell attempted some clumsy damage control, claiming that he "could not account" for the hippo prints. This was an interesting response, considering one particular item in his possession: a large, silver-plated ashtray made from the stuffed foot of a hippopotamus.

Marmaduke Wetherell had faked the prints.

Wetherell's hippo foot ashtray

CHAPTER 12

PLOT

Is it "possible for a hippo to live in the chill waters of Northern Scotland?
    Our reply is, we ha' our doots!"
                            —*Northern Whig*, January 13, 1934

Marmaduke Wetherell had gotten the chance of a lifetime. He'd been hired for one of the world's most publicized stunts—and he'd bungled it, badly. It wasn't just that he'd faked evidence. He'd been *caught* trying to pass that evidence off as real. A week after Calman's letter identified the footprints as belonging to a dried hippo foot, the word "hoax" began circulating in Scottish papers. One Scotsman wrote into his local paper, bemoaning the ridiculous state of affairs. "Lochnessity is the mother of invention," he sighed. Then he asked "Are we all victims of a gigantic hoax?"

At first, people assumed that Wetherell had been a victim of someone else's prank. They thought that another set of hoaxers had placed the prints, and he'd simply been fooled by them. While this was probably better than being blamed for his own tomfoolery, it still painted an unflattering picture of Wetherell.

This was a man who'd hunted lions and shot crocodiles. How could he have confused a monster print with a hippo's?

All of Wetherell's early efforts to document his monster hunt now made things worse for him. Newspaper readers knew his name. They knew his movies. They knew his photo. He was now tied to a mismanaged prank. But while Wetherell's reputation crumbled, the world remained steadfastly excited about the possibility of the Loch Ness Monster. They snickered at Wetherell but kept their eyes glued to the loch. There *could* still be a monster out there. The *Daily Mail* pushed this narrative. On the same day that the paper published Calman's verdict on the hippo prints, it ran an article about a group of students who had discovered a footprint of their own on a different part of the shoreline. It was as if the *Mail* was waving something shiny at its readers, urging them to forget the Wetherell nonsense and instead, "look over here!"

The *Mail* had plenty of ways to distract its readers from the hippo hoax. Two days later, it reported on yet another monster sighting. This one had taken place at about one a.m. on January 4 while veterinary student Arthur Grant was riding home from a party on his motorcycle. Grant claimed to have seen a huge animal burst onto the road in front of him. He said it crossed the pavement in two swift bounds before flopping itself down the shore and into the water. Grant estimated the monster was about twenty feet long. He said it had a long, strong tail. Then he added that it had jaws that would "easily hold a lamb or goat." This clearly recalled George Spicer's monster sighting from the previous summer. It suggested one of two scenarios: Grant had seen Spicer's beast, or Grant was imitating Spicer's story. The latter became far more likely when another detail emerged.

Shortly after reporting his monster encounter, a man overheard Grant telling a friend, "They've swallowed it."

Wetherell heard Grant's story and jumped at the chance to redeem himself. He and Pauli traveled to the site of Grant's encounter the next morning. There, they claimed to happen upon an odd assortment of evidence. They found a three-toed footprint, a pile of bones, and a ragged bit of sheep's skin. Wetherell and Pauli took turns posing for pictures with Grant and the sheepskin, each holding a tiny magnifying glass and looking studious. If Wetherell thought this photo shoot would redeem his reputation, he was wrong. When the *Dundee Courier*, printed the image, it cropped Wetherell and Pauli out entirely.

Around this time, the old theory that the monster was just a large seal resurfaced. This explanation made plenty of sense. A seal's head looked a bit like the snake-dog-horse creature so often described by witnesses, and its back could certainly resemble one of the monster's famed "humps." Tales from local fishers backed this theory up. Recently, they had been hauling in salmon that looked as though they'd been chewed by seals. In a bold about-face, Wetherell even jumped onto this trend. On January 16, he told the *Daily Mail* that he had spotted "a very big seal" in the loch. It left "no room for doubt" in the big-game hunter's mind: there was no monster. The beast was a seal.

This seal theory put the *Daily Mail* in a tough spot. If the loch creature was indeed a simple seal, then the drama and intrigue of the monster hunt would be over. Journalists handled the issue with care. They reported on the disappointing seal narrative, but made sure to leave the matter open-ended for their readers. The *Mail* concluded a January 19 article about the seal theory with

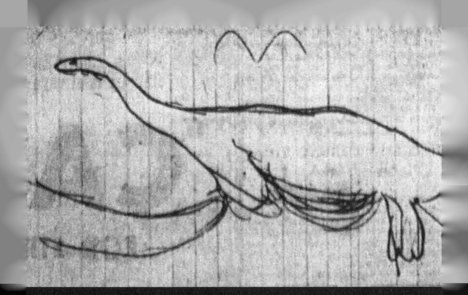

Sketch by Arthur Grant, showing the creature he witnessed

Grant and Pauli pose for photos with their odd discoveries

a well-known reverend's opposition to it. He felt "absolutely convinced" that "a weird and mysterious creature does really and truly haunt these deep waters." The paper covered its bases, telling readers that sure, the creature *might* be a seal, but odds were still good that it was a monster.

While the *Mail* did this dance, competing newspapers delighted in covering the hippo-foot scandal. *Reynolds's* newspaper ran a gleeful piece entitled "Hip-Hip-O For the Monster" that highlighted the whole sordid affair. The *Inverness Courier* printed a scorching editorial about the way the "gutter-press" had handled the Loch Ness Monster saga, pointing at "the depths to which some so-called newspapers can descend." Other papers piled on. The *Hull Daily Mail* ran a piece in which a local museum director named Mr. T. Sheppard used an elephant foot trash can to create footprints of his own. A photographer followed along as Sheppard carefully pressed the elephant foot into sandy ground, creating perfectly monstrous tracks. The paper didn't mention Wetherell by name, but it didn't need to. The whole article was clearly making fun of him, including a series of photos that were strikingly similar to those the *Daily Mail* printed of Wetherell. Sheppard even resembled the big-game hunter, standing on a rocky shoreline in a hat and trench coat, with a cigarette dangling from his lips. The article concluded with a snarky summary: "It just shows, doesn't it, how the game of hokos-pokus, whackferlayree-laddio can be played upon the public if you only have a practical joker with imagination and a waste-paper basket made out of an elephant's foot." The implication was clear. Wetherell was the practical joker.

Other jokers soon got in on the fun. Shortly after the hippo-foot revelation became public, popular funnyman John Tilley released a comedy album called *The Loch Ness Monster*. In it, he mocks a man who spent his morning making monster footprints on the shore. The album had people all over the UK clutching their sides from laughter, a great moment for Tilley and a regrettable one for Wetherell.

Reynolds's followed with another stab at Wetherell, playing up a rivalry between the big-game hunter and the museum officials who'd debunked his hoax. It quoted a zoologist from the British Museum who said, "You have to choose between Mr. Wetherell and us." Newspapers were drawing a line in the sand. On one side were rational, logical thinkers and on the other was Wetherell. Whichever side readers chose, the newspapers won because people were buying them.

Wetherell found himself in an unusual situation. The very paper that had elevated his name was now the reason it was being ridiculed. And while other newspapers gleefully poked fun at him, the *Mail* slowly distanced itself from the big-game hunter. The near-daily coverage of the *Mail*'s monster hunt, which had, in its early days, made Wetherell the focus, had shrunk drastically and pivoted away from him. For example, on January 1, 1934, the *Mail* devoted two full columns to the hunt and mentioned Wetherell multiple times. As the days went on, coverage of Wetherell diminished, and the spotlight shifted elsewhere. The last time his name appeared in the hunt coverage was January 17. By January 22, the story was down to a tiny blurb.

Wetherell didn't want to let the *Mail* just slink away. This whole ordeal was the *Mail*'s doing. The paper had hired him, publicized his work, and pressured him to find evidence of the beast. Any false information that had made it into print was the *Mail*'s fault, not Wetherell's. It was time for revenge. "All right," he said to his son, Ian. "We'll give them their monster." With those five words, the plans for the greatest monster hoax of all time were born.

CHAPTER 13

HOAX

In early 1934, Marmaduke Wetherell came up with a plan. He would fake an elaborate monster photo to get back at the *Daily Mail* for all the trouble it had caused. He'd light the photo perfectly, stage it flawlessly, and make it look as real as possible. Then, he'd pass it to the *Mail*. If all went well, editors would believe the photo was real and run it in the paper. Wetherell would have the last laugh, knowing that he'd fooled those pesky editors at the *Daily Mail*. For once, it wouldn't just be the readers being duped by a phony story. The editors would be fooled, too.

It's hard to imagine a man better suited for such a task. Wetherell, an experienced film director and actor, knew how to stage a scene. He knew about lighting, perspective, props, and background. He knew what audiences needed to see in order to understand a story. This had been especially important in his many silent films. Without dialogue, Wetherell had been forced to communicate entirely through visual clues. In addition to his scene-setting expertise, Wetherell also had a fair amount of experience in stretching the truth. His stories were great, "but most of them came out of his brain," his stepson Christian

Spurling later recalled. "If Wetherell shot one elephant before breakfast, by the time it was twelve o'clock it was three elephants."

Ian Wetherell

Wetherell wouldn't have to work alone. He had two family members who were well equipped to help. His son, twenty-two-year-old Ian, was his first recruit and an excellent coconspirator. Ian had clearly inherited his father's storytelling skills. "He was a great raconteur," his son would later say, "he kept everyone amused." Ian could weave a story so artfully he'd captivate an entire room. This skill had come in handy in his acting career, of course, but now it would help as the pair concocted their devious plot. Ian's time on the stage had also helped him learn the importance of staging; props and background mattered when putting on a performance. And they were about to put on the performance of a lifetime.

Neither Ian nor his father had the special effects skills needed for this project. Wetherell reached out to Spurling for help. Spurling, twenty-nine, was a cameraman, a painter, and, more importantly, a talented model maker. Though he spent most of his time recreating famous tall ships, Spurling knew how to build other realistic models, too. Wetherell asked him, "Can you make me a monster?" Spurling said sure, and the group of pranksters grew to three.

Ian went to a local Woolworth's department store and spent a couple of shillings on a child's toy submarine. He gave it to Spurling to be transformed into a miniature monster. Not knowing exactly how the creature should look, Spurling got creative. He thought, "Well, a monster, it's got to have a long neck I suppose." He added layers of plastic wood to the submarine to form a long, arching neck, much like what he imagined a sea serpent might have. When the sculpture had dried, he carefully sanded it down to make it smooth, then painted it gray. His experience building model ships had taught Spurling that his creation wouldn't float as it was. The sculpted neck would make the model top-heavy. He added a lead counterweight to the bottom. This allowed the contraption to bob atop the water, neck held high, without capsizing. After eight days of work, he gave it to Wetherell.

"The old man was very pleased with it," Spurling remembered.

Maurice Chambers

The Wetherells had their monster. Now they needed something to capture it with. They turned to a London friend named Maurice Chambers. The perfect accomplice for such a prank, Chambers was a colorful character who rubbed shoulders with London's "it" crowd, drove a yellow Rolls-Royce, and, luckily, happened to own a state-of-the-art camera. He loaned it to the Wetherells, thus linking himself to the hijinks. The band of pranksters swelled to four.

Ian and his father packed the model monster and Chambers's camera into their car and set off for Scotland. Handsome and neat, with short, oiled hair combed straight back from his angular face, Ian had a reputation for loving go-carts and luxury cars and for driving far too fast. Under his lead foot, the pair zipped up to Loch Ness and began location scouting. In the same way a movie director needs the perfect setting for each scene, the Wetherell men needed a specific backdrop for their planned picture. It couldn't be too busy. If anyone saw what they were up to, they'd be busted. The setting also needed to show some identifiable landmarks so that there could be no question about where the photo had been taken. Finally, the setting had to work for a very small monster. Spurling's model was only about fourteen inches long. This meant that it had to float relatively close to the shoreline so that it didn't look tiny in the photograph.

The pair soon hit the jackpot. Ian later recalled, "We found an inlet where the tiny ripples would look like full-size waves out in the loch, and with the actual scenery in the background." They made their way down to the rocky shoreline and sent the model monster floating out into the water. As it bobbed and wobbled on the loch's surface, Ian snapped five photographs with the borrowed camera. The whole plan nearly collapsed when a passerby approached the inlet, but a quick-thinking Wetherell sank the model by stomping on it with his foot, sending it to the loch's dark bottom.

Monster mischief complete, the father-son duo now needed to grow their band of hoaxers one last time. The Wetherells had what they wanted: a set of photos purporting to show the Loch Ness Monster. But they couldn't claim ownership of the pictures. Marmaduke's name was still fresh in the minds of *Daily Mail* readers, and it would look suspicious if the photos were linked to him. Likewise, Ian couldn't say they were his because of his last name. Spurling couldn't be roped in either. It would be far too easy for a plucky reporter to realize he was Wetherell's stepson. Luckily, Wetherell's background in film had taught him exactly how to cast the perfect actor for a role. He soon found his leading man in a fellow named Robert Kenneth Wilson. A veteran of the First World War, Wilson was a London physician with a dizzying string of credentials that followed his name: MA, MBChB Camb., FRCS. He had the right look, too. Wilson was clean-cut, with a trimmed mustache and a hesitant smile. He looked remarkably normal. Only those closest to him knew the real truth. "R.K. was a great prankster with a wicked sense of humor," a friend later admitted. Wilson agreed to join in on the fun, the fifth and final member of the band of pranksters.

On April 19, 1934, Wilson drove the film to Loch Ness to be developed at a local shop. The shopkeeper looked at the film and asked, "You haven't got the Loch Ness Monster, have you?" Wilson replied that, actually, he might have. It was an Oscar-worthy scene. One can almost imagine Wetherell sitting nearby in a director's chair, patting his cameraman on the back and grinning.

Dr. Robert Kenneth Wilson

Hours later, the photos were ready. When Wilson arrived to pick them up, the shopkeeper was stunned. He handed the doctor a black-and-white image which clearly showed the head and neck of a dark creature arching gracefully over a rippling pool of water. It was magnificent! He then issued some stern advice. Wilson should get himself over to the *Daily Mail*, stat. The world needed to see this.

Wilson, doing a marvelous acting job, followed the shopkeeper's directions. He took the photograph straight over to the *Daily Mail*, where a gobsmacked editor purchased it for immediate use.

On April 21, 1934, the *Daily Mail* printed the photo and the world turned upside down.

CHAPTER 14

SUCCESS

L ight drizzle fell across London. As the city grew slick with rain, Londoners bustled to and fro under darkening trench coats and black umbrellas. Near Fleet Street, London's printing and publishing epicenter, stood the Northcliffe House. The imposing gray stone building looked still and sullen from the outside, like a sleeping giant. On the inside, it was a buzzing architectural and technological marvel, and home to the *Daily Mail*. Built specifically for newspaper production, it housed mammoth printing presses in its basement, capable of churning out an unrivaled two million, twenty-page papers in a single day. Upstairs, a hive of workers occupied two hundred desks, one hundred tables, and one hundred typewriters. Urgent messages zoomed into newsrooms via pneumatic tubes and overhead zip lines. These ensured that the *Daily Mail* delivered the freshest, most up-to-date news stories. That morning, as editors filed to their desks, the air smelled of ink, fresh paper and *success*. It was April 21, 1934, and the *Mail* had just printed the photo of the century.

Hours earlier, readers had been astounded to see a banner of huge, bold text stretched across the page 11 of the day's paper.

The "Surgeon's Photo," taken by Dr. R. K. Wilson

The headline bellowed, "WEST END SURGEON'S PHOTO OF THE MONSTER." Underneath was a cropped version of Dr. R. K. Wilson's monster snap, which appeared to show an honest-to-goodness lake monster. Mixed in with the pitter-patter of the morning's rain was the thunk-thunk-thunk of jaws hitting the floor across London as people absorbed the news.

The article below the photograph told readers all about the lucky doctor who had chanced upon a monster. It featured Wilson's own made-up description of the event. It told how he had spotted a "sudden commotion" in the loch, then hurried to snap several photos before watching the monster's head slowly "sink from view." It was an entertaining read, with the most exciting details printed in bold. This made it easy for busy readers to simply scan the text and take away the most sensational points. The article also did a fair amount of gloating, informing readers that the *Daily Mail* was the first to break the story, and the first to secure an interview with Wilson.

Editors at the *Mail* probably didn't think that the image, which would soon be known as the "surgeon's photograph," was a hoax. Wilson's story and demeanor were perfectly convincing. Plus, the night before the paper printed the image, a *Daily Mail* journalist took the photo to three experts for their opinions. Rather than discounting it, they said "it was like nothing they had ever seen before." As if to emphasize its importance, a second, enlarged version of the surgeon's photo appeared on the back page of the paper. This invited study, scrutiny, and excitement. The *Daily Mail*'s handling of this bombshell image pushed two lies onto its readers: the photograph was real, and the Loch Ness Monster was real. The two lies were followed by a single truth: the *Daily Mail* was still a news powerhouse.

Nabbing the extraordinary monster photo marked a huge triumph for the paper, not just because it gave the *Mail* a leg up on its competition. It also helped nudge the troubling hippo-foot fiasco into the recesses of the public's memory.

In the days that followed, editors at rival British newspapers hurried to get their hands on copies of the surgeon's photo, too. Papers outside of the UK soon followed suit. Fortunately, a new technology called phototelegraphy had just emerged. This made it possible to share photos quickly and over long distances. Phototelegraphy was a complicated process by which photographs could be scanned, translated from light into energy, and then sent through telephone wires. The recipient could, utilizing a slew of little glass bulbs, rotating cylinders, and buzzing wires, print out a copy of the photograph herself. It used to take days or weeks to send a photograph across the ocean. Phototelegraphy meant that photos could be shared in a matter of minutes. As word of the surgeon's photo spread, so too did the need for readers to see it with their own eyes. Phototelegraphy enabled newspaper editors to meet that need. Phone wires buzzed as the image crossed oceans and continents, landing on all manner of front pages. Around the world, eyes bulged. One New York man saw the photo and declared, "the Scotch monster really exists," and that it was a sign that people needed to open their minds and expand their worldviews. "This seems to be an era of readjustment of all sorts of ideas," he exclaimed, "including our ideas about sea beasts."

Not everyone wanted their ideas readjusted. Some members of the scientific community remained skeptical. A German zoologist huffed in annoyance. The photo didn't show a monster, he scowled. It showed an ordinary dolphin! The curator of the British Sea Anglers reached a similar conclusion. He decided that the photo actually showed "the dorsal fin of an old male killer whale." The keeper of zoology at South Kensington shrugged, "May be a diving bird." William Calman, the British Museum zoologist who had figured out Wetherell's hippo-foot scam, agreed. He thought perhaps Wilson had just snapped a photo at the precise moment a bird dipped into the water. He even suggested a breed, the crested grebe.

Just down the hall from Calman's office, a nameless colleague disagreed. He thought that the monster was real. He also believed that the museum should stake a claim to it soon before it could be snatched up by a rival museum. In the spring of 1934, he took his interest in the monster to the next level and wrote a

Sketch drawn by the curator of the British Sea Anglers suggesting that the Surgeon's Photo likely captured a killer whale.

letter to a bounty hunter, urging him to catch the beast: "Should you ever come within range of the 'monster' I hope you will not be deterred by humanitarian considerations from shooting him on the spot and sending the carcass to us in cold storage, carriage forward." The unnamed museum worker went on, noting that the hunter shouldn't panic if he couldn't snag the beast's entire corpse: "a flipper, a jaw or a tooth would be very welcome." Four hundred miles to the north, officials at the Royal Scottish Museum in Edinburgh began to worry that their prized monster might be snatched away to London. They penned a letter to Scotland's secretary of state, Sir Godfrey Collins. In it, they urged him to give them "rights to the 'Monster' if and when its corpse should become available."

Loch Ness Monster mania had reached a boiling point. While the world squinted at a grainy black-and-white photo purporting to show the beast, two of the most prestigious museums in all of the United Kingdom were quietly plotting to get their hands on its corpse. Ever the loyal Scot, Sir Godfrey sided with the Royal Scottish Museum. "We think the Monster should not be allowed to find its last resting place in England," he wrote. "Such a fate would surely outrage Scottish nationalism which at the moment is thriving greatly under the Monster's beneficent influence." Sir Godfrey liked what the Loch Ness Monster had done for Scotland's economy and spirit. He wasn't going to let the English steal its body.

Indeed, business around Loch Ness was better than ever. Just one day after the surgeon's photograph appeared in the *Daily Mail*, the paper reported that "thousands of people visited the loch hoping to catch a glimpse of the monster," noting that "a line of motor cars travelled down both sides of the loch."

Throughout the excitement that followed the publication of their photograph, the Wetherell men remained silent. This was probably out of necessity. If Marmaduke, his son, or his stepson had publicly claimed involvement with the photo, the whole prank would have come crumbling down. Wetherell's reputation had been dragged through the mud. Any association with the photograph would muddy its believability, too.

In contrast, Dr. Wilson continued to give the public performance of a lifetime. When reporters hounded him for details, he acted as shocked as everyone else about what he'd photographed. Just as a professional doctor wouldn't make reckless guesses about a patient's diagnosis, Wilson refused to speculate, conjecture, or theorize about the monster. He remained humble, confessing that he was "inexperienced as a photographer and was, in fact, very much of the amateur." He told a reporter, "I am not able to describe clearly what I saw, as I was so busy taking the snaps, and when I had finished the object moved a little and submerged." Even this was telling. He hesitated to call the subject of his photograph a monster, preferring instead to say "the object," as though he were patiently waiting for scientific proof otherwise. Unlike Wetherell, who had broadcast every detail of his expedition to Loch Ness, Wilson seemed to shy away from the limelight. His reticence made the story all the more believable. Many people read his halting, awkward interviews and thought, *he's telling the truth*.

While scores of people gaped at the surgeon's photo as proof of the monster's existence, one American man looked at the image and felt a shock of recognition. H. W. Watrous, an eighty-year-old designer, had pulled off a sea serpent stunt of his own thirty years earlier. In 1904, hoping to have some "good-natured fun," Watrous had carved a cedar log into the shape of a monster, then floated it out into New York's Lake George. He attached it to a rope and weighted pulley so that he could lower and raise the monster. When his friends approached in a boat, Watrous released the rope, sending the monster bobbing to the surface. His friends were terrified. It was great. Watrous pulled the stunt several times, causing rumors of a sea monster to spread like wildfire around Lake George. Some residents of the lake became so scared that they actually moved away. All these memories came flooding back to Watrous when he saw the surgeon's photo. He had to come clean. He also wanted to share his suspicion that the "Scots were 'spoofing' the world in like manner" to what he'd done all those years earlier. Watrous spilled the beans to the *New York Times*, and the world soon learned of his trickery. But despite Watrous's confession, and the very obvious similarities to the events in Loch Ness, monster fever burned on. People loved the monster story so much that many simply weren't interested in exploring evidence against it.

Wetherell must have felt conflicted about the public response to the surgeon's photo. The entire world was looking at his art. They were captivated, energized, and terrified. And they attributed it all to Wilson, not Wetherell. But while he might have felt shortchanged about not getting credit for his work, he was probably satisfied with at least one component of the prank's success: revenge. He'd fooled the *Daily Mail* with a perfectly believable monster, and the *Daily Mail* shared it with the world. This was his goal all along, after all. Wetherell had been slighted by a major newspaper, and, in turn, he got in in a good jab of his own.

But Wetherell and his co-conspirators never could have imagined just how far their little prank would go. The surgeon's photograph went on to appear on the front page of magazines and newspapers on every continent.

CHAPTER 15

NESSIE

As the Loch Ness Monster approached her first birthday, poverty continued to plague much of the global population. With it came desperation and crime. In America, where 3,600 banks had gone belly-up and nearly one-third of households didn't have a single employed resident, lawlessness occasionally prevailed. Mob bosses governed major cities like Chicago and New York. Bootlegging, robbery, and even murder were frighteningly common. Franklin D. Roosevelt began his American presidency with the dire statement: "Only a foolish optimist can deny the dark realities of the moment." Elsewhere, disorder and upheaval ruled. Crime in England was on a meteoric rise. It had *quintupled* in the previous five years. Politics, too, were in turmoil. In 1934 alone, Yugoslavia's King Alexander I, Austria's Chancellor Engelbert Dollfuss, and the Soviet Union's First Secretary of Leningrad, Sergei Kirov, were assassinated.

It was against this backdrop that the surgeon's photo appeared in the spring of 1934. Though it purported to show a fearsome beast, the photo itself was a welcome relief for a weary, on-edge, heartsick world. The Loch Ness Monster gave people from all over the planet something else to think about. *A monster!* Adding to the monster's crowd appeal was its supposed temperament. Witnesses described it as shy, quiet, and, above all, nonviolent. It didn't want to cause anyone pain (other than the area's fishers, whose salmon it would surely deplete). It was the mascot no one knew they needed, but that united the crowds nonetheless.

People embraced the monster as a treasured savior, a torch that lit their gloomy world. The affection they felt for the beast showed in the way they talked about it. In early 1934, people started calling it Nessie. This cute, cuddly nickname sent a clear message about the creature's persona. Nessie may have been a monster, but she was a *beloved* monster. When a Benedictine monk claimed to have seen the beast in May 1934, he used adoring terms to describe it. It was "not the fearsome thing some have declared," he said, "but a graceful creature" with a "beautifully shaped" head. This adoring attitude became so widespread that it even reached England's royal family. "The other day I was in the nursery," Prince Albert, Duke of York told a banquet audience in 1934, "and my younger daughter, [Princess] Margaret Rose, aged three, was looking at a fairy story picture book. She came across a picture of a dragon. Pointing at the picture, she said: 'Oh, look . . . what a darling little Loch Ness Monster.'"

Other signs of Nessie love began popping up in unexpected ways and places. Just nine days after the surgeon's photo was first published, women in Paris began chatting about a trendy new outfit called the "Loch Ness." It included "a slender dark green wool frock with a hip-length jacket of the same fabric designed with long front 'tails' furred in gray fox. It is accompanied by a narrow brimmed hat of dark green felt with a fluff of the same gray fur on top of the crown." Other fashions that year also reflected the excitement in Scotland. Stylish French women wore beautiful silk frocks covered "with weird picturesque animal designs," which were "inspired by 'le Montre de Loch Ness.'" For those who weren't willing to commit to an entirely green ensemble, an easier fashion trend also flourished. Women wore tiny gold or silver Nessie charms on necklaces.

Fashion wasn't the only way to show one's love for the beast. Children in Bathgate, Scotland, honored Nessie by enthusiastically gobbling her down. A resourceful baker there had begun churning out boatloads of monster-shaped gingerbread cookies. Customers scooped them up by the fistful. In St. Andrews, Scotland, a different baker fashioned little Nessie-shaped loaves of brown bread, promising fresh, hot lake monsters each day for just 1 pence apiece. These culinary tributes soon spread beyond Scotland's borders. In London, a fine dining chef presented his guests with "Le Filet de Sole 'Loch Ness.'" This monster entrée included a baked potato and sole "body," lobster claw "flippers," and a walnut "head." The whole thing arrived swimming in a green sauce. *Voilà.*

These little nods to Nessie reflected not only a general affection for the monster, but also a familiarity that came from her regular appearance in the news. People might not have known every detail about the hunt for the Loch Ness Monster, but they knew of her existence. And, thanks to the surgeon's photo, they knew what she looked like. Nessie had a long neck and small head. Though it wasn't visible in the photo, people assumed that below the water was a large, flippered body. From 1934 onward, this image of the Loch Ness Monster would stick.

One month after the surgeon's photo was printed, the British film, *Secret of the Loch*, hit theaters. Thrown together with admirable gusto but a miniscule budget, it wasn't very good. Unlike the special effects team behind *King Kong*, who had labored endlessly over stop-motion models, the filmmakers of *The Secret of the Loch* had simply plopped a live iguana in front of the camera. The lizard scampered around a bit on camera while a scuba-diving monster hunter cowered dramatically. The result, as the film's writer admitted, was "terrible . . . but amusing." Audiences didn't care. It was a movie about their favorite monster! Film critics, clearly caught up in the frenzy, were extremely kind in their reviews, with one even labeling it "sensational."

The following month, Rupert Gould published his book *The Loch Ness Monster and Others*. In it, the motorcycling author and expert on nearly everything declared that Nessie was real. Gould's endorsement served as further proof that Highlanders weren't making any of this up. They were telling the truth, and their stories were spectacular.

Hoping to get the scoop on some of the more fantastic stories, foreign journalists and politicians swarmed the area from Japan, France, Denmark, and elsewhere. Visitors peered at the loch and crossed their fingers that they'd be one of the lucky few who could leave Scotland with not just a Nessie souvenir, but a real sighting as well. This optimism spread, and soon people who weren't anywhere near the Highlands began to see Loch Ness Monster knockoffs in their own rivers, streams, lakes, and seas. Nessie's kin were spotted in France, Turkey, Italy, Canada, Germany, Southern Rhodesia (Zimbabwe) and more. A hotel owner on the Danube River one-upped everyone, claiming that he'd seen a monster of his own, though it was "larger than the one . . . in Loch Ness." This beast made tracks like an elephant and turned the tourist season into a "colossal success" for the shrewd businessman.

The affection for Nessie wasn't just a reaction to the dismal state of world politics and national economies. It was also the result of a phenomenon described by P. T. Barnum, American circus owner. Barnum had made a towering career out of staging incredible shows filled with true wonders (acrobats leaping through the air) and false ones (tricks facilitated by smoke and mirrors). He knew that his audiences were just as entertained by his bogus tricks as his real ones, and he was famous for claiming that "the public likes to be fooled." Barnum clarified in his autobiography, writing that "the public appears disposed to be amused even when they are conscious of being deceived." In other words, people don't mind being duped when it is entertaining.

P. T. Barnum's boastful statement points to an important part of the Loch Ness Monster story: many people who didn't believe in Nessie still found enjoyment in the surrounding mythology. These skeptics could poke holes in an eyewitness account or stare critically at the surgeon's photo *and* enjoy the resulting buzz at the same time. Just because someone didn't believe in the monster didn't mean they disapproved of her. Nessie brought so much money, interest, and enthusiasm to Loch Ness that it was hard to hold a grudge against her. Nessie might have been a big fat dupe, but she was a fun dupe.

London's *Daily Herald* acknowledged this, calling the excitement around Loch Ness a "monster racket," and declaring that Scottish people "fear only one thing more than the monster being at large—and that is that it might be caught." In late May, that fear was nearly realized when a Scottish fisherman claimed to have caught the monster in the waters of Moray Firth, a bay located just a few miles up the River Ness from Loch Ness. The beast he hauled from the bay was odd, indeed. It had silvery gray scales and a snakelike body, with a thin, pointed head, and large eyes. Crowds of people rushed to the area to behold the specimen and issue their verdict. Some squinted at the corpse on the ground and shrugged, suggesting that it *could* be the beast. They supposed that the long, narrow body might have moved in a way that created the telltale humps in the water, or the arching neck and head from the surgeon's photograph. Others disagreed. This wasn't their monster. It was the wrong color, shape, and size. Scientists agreed with the naysayers, declaring that the fisherman's epic catch was actually just a big oarfish. At this, monster lovers exhaled in relief. If this wasn't the monster, then the monster was still out there. And if the monster was still out there, then monster sightings, monster tourism, and monster fever would rage on.

CHAPTER 16

THEORIES

"Every legend has a basis of truth."

—*King Kong*, 1933

W ith the surgeon's photograph in hand, people finally had the answer to one burning question: yes, a monster did live in Loch Ness. Now they had to contend with a flood of follow-up questions, just as burning and just as difficult to answer: *What was it? When and how did it get there?* And of course, *why now?* There was still no physical proof for scientists to examine—no body, bones, prints, or skin. All anyone had were a few terrible images, R. K. Wilson's superior snap, and more than one hundred eyewitness accounts. This meant that answering questions about the monster required a fair amount of creativity and guesswork. Theories sprouted like wildflowers on a Scottish hillside, and newspapers printed just about all of them.

A popular theory about Nessie's identity claimed that she was a plesiosaur, a type of prehistoric marine reptile that had lived in seas and oceans all around the planet back in the age of dinosaurs. Plesiosaurs had barrel-shaped bodies, flippered limbs, long necks, and small heads. Unfortunately for pro-plesiosaurians, there wasn't much to this theory beyond a resemblance to the creature in the surgeon's photo. Plesiosaurs went extinct sixty-five million years ago. In addition, the loch had likely formed only about ten thousand years ago. This meant that a gap of 64,990,000 years existed between when the last plesiosaur took its final paddle and when Loch Ness first started to fill with water. Even without this pesky timeline issue, there was another key reason that the plesiosaur theory didn't hold up. That kind of continued presence in a body of water would have produced mounds of evidence. Over the years, bones would have washed ashore. Rotting carcasses would have floated to the surface. Fishermen would have pulled a monster in with a net. None of that had happened, suggesting that the plesiosaur idea was nothing more than wishful thinking. In spite of this, papers ran dozens of articles pushing it.

Other less popular theories about the monster's identity focused on modern animals, such as the suggestion that the Nessie was actually just a rogue killer whale who'd wound up in the Highland loch. This idea didn't impress many. Killer whales were too big to sneak into such a loch without being seen. Plus, they breathe air in great, puffing gasps. Surely someone would have seen or heard it. "Besides," one scientist pointed out, a killer whale is "a most voracious creature." If one were in the lake, "it would be given away at once by fish jumping all over the place to escape" it. Other theories of animal misidentification were also proposed: it was a seal, an otter, a diving bird, a squid, or an eel.

A handful of non-animal explanations for Nessie were thrown around, too. An American shipping executive swore that the monster was actually just the wreckage of a German blimp that had been shot down during WWI. The problem with this theory was that no blimps had actually been shot down over Loch Ness. Some suggested that big chunks of rotting vegetation, made buoyant by bubbles of gas trapped inside, had risen to the loch's surface and fooled people into thinking they'd seen a monster. Like the other theories, this one failed to explain many of the sightings, including the creature from the surgeon's photo, since decomposing plant matter was unlikely to look like a head and neck rising over the water.

Setting aside the question of *what* Nessie was, many people chose to focus their attention on the issue of *how* and *when* she got into the loch. A popular explanation suggested that Nessie had simply made her way into the loch from the ocean via the Caledonian Canal. This is a long stretch of water that cuts across Scotland from Inverness to Fort William through a series of lakes and human-made narrow waterways. This theory wasn't perfect. Parts of the canal are quite shallow. Nessie would have had to be young and small to fit through it. There are also a series of locks built into the canal to control water levels for boat traffic. This meant that, along her journey, the Loch Ness Monster would have had to belly flop over various obstacles. In addition to being a rather difficult task for a bulky sea monster, it also would have drawn the attention of anyone nearby. The only way for the Caledonian Canal theory to work would have been if Nessie had made her way up the canal as a little baby and in the dead of night.

Taking note of the difficulty involved in a trip down the Caledonian Canal, some monster fans suggested an alternate route. They wondered if there might be a system of subterranean tunnels that connect the loch to the ocean, and, if so, whether Nessie might have found her way through them and into her new home. This suggestion conjured an incredible scene: a massive water monster gliding through inky tunnels, maneuvering bends and dips in rocky passageways, and then emerging in the depths of Loch Ness. Like the Caledonian Canal theory, this subterranean version had as many holes as a leaky ship. A tunnel would have to stretch all the way to the North Sea, a distance of at least seven and a half miles. This would make it almost twice the length of the world's largest known cave, Vietnam's Hang Sơn Đoòng. The tunnel theory also didn't make much sense when considering the level of Loch Ness's water. If Loch Ness connected to the sea via tunnels, then their water levels would match. Instead, Loch Ness's water level remains stubbornly high, measuring roughly fifty-two feet above sea level. To explain this difference in level, some ardent tunnel theorizers came up with an explanation one researcher has called "generally improbable to the point of daftness." They suggest that the tunnels contain an upside-down U-bend, sort of like the pipes in a toilet, that rises high enough to allow a portion of the cavern to remain dry before dropping back down into the water. This would explain the difference in water levels between the loch and the sea, but it would also require any migrating monsters to trek at least a portion of their journey on dry tunnel floors, a rough trip for a flippered beast.

The toilet-bend-tunnel theory was dubious, but it was nothing compared to another theory that emerged. After the surgeon's photo release inspired copycat monster sightings around the world, imaginative scientists attempted to explain the sudden appearance of so many water beasts. A South African paper printed one group's outrageous suggestion that the monster "'epidemic' was probably caused by an undersea volcano, which spouted the creatures to the surface." This theory suggested that a family of Nessies had been paddling along the ocean floor when a sudden deep-sea eruption sent them all rocketing skyward. One plunked down in Canada, while others splashed down in Germany, Italy, and, of course, Scotland.

In searching for a rational explanation for the Loch Ness Monster's existence, a nagging question continued to pop up: why had monster sightings only just begun in 1933? Many locals answered this question by pointing their fingers at a recent construction project. In 1933, the road that ran along the north shore of the loch had been repaired and resurfaced. They suggested that the noise and disruption caused by the road repair had disturbed a previously dormant monster, prompting it to rise to the surface. Nessie was just a light sleeper! This theory raised more questions, such as why the monster hadn't appeared during other noisy loch side building projects.

Others argued that the monster sightings weren't new at all. Rather, they'd been happening for years and nobody had paid them any mind. They scoured their memories and piles of yellowing newspaper clippings for stories about big fish or unusual waves, pointing to each as evidence of monster activity. They pointed to a 1930 incident in which three fishermen saw a big fish moving in a "wiggling motion" in the loch. They also remembered the 1932 drowning of Winifred Hambro in Loch Ness. Had the monster been behind both incidents? They argued that it was possible.

Looking deeper into history, enthusiastic Nessie fans found even more evidence for a monstrous presence in Loch Ness.

They pointed to an ancient story about Saint Columba, who had visited the area in 564 CE on a quest to convert as many Scots as possible to Christianity. Apparently, while preparing to cross the River Ness, one of the saint's followers had had a run-in with a river beast. The creature gave "an awful roar" and "darted after" the man "with its mouth wide open." Columba, watching the whole fiasco from the shore, invoked the name of God and made the sign of the cross in the air. He bellowed to the monster, "Thou shalt go no further, nor touch the man; go back with all speed." The suddenly frightened monster made a beeline for the depths.

For centuries, this story about Saint Columba had been taught as a lesson about faith. If you believed in God's protection, then you could face anything, even a ravenous river monster. But as Loch Ness Monster stories gained traction, people began to think more about this ancient tale. Was it an early eyewitness account of the Loch Ness Monster? It didn't sound much like the placid, shy beast of modern times. Still, some Nessie fans thought it was close enough. Linking Nessie to such a distant past strengthened her legitimacy. It also gave modern people an idea of how they might handle Nessie should she ever become dangerous. As one Scottish official wrote in 1934, Saint Columba's treatment "seems to have been fairly effective for upwards of 1,300 years." This was a lesson for readers: if Nessie ever attacked, they just needed to make the sign of the cross and shout the Lord's name.

Nessie lovers also worked to connect the monster to a group of Scottish mythical creatures called kelpies. Prominent in local folklore, kelpies were deadly, shape-shifting water creatures that often took the form of horses. Any child who climbed onto a kelpie's back would find herself fused to its skin, unable to dismount, even as the kelpie dove under the water. Legend told of scores of children disappearing on the backs of kelpies, pulled to their watery deaths. While terrifying, kelpies also seemed fairly commonplace. In 1812, a Scottish clergyman named Patrick Graham wrote that "Every lake has its kelpie or water-horse, often seen by the shepherd sitting upon the brow of a rock, dashing along the surface of the deep, or browsing upon the pasture on its verge." The idea that Nessie was a kelpie quickly gained traction among reporters and newspaper readers. Outsiders picked up on this theory and ran with it, managing to be both condescending and excited at the same time. A Minnesota paper reported that kelpie legends were usually "ascribed to the vivid imagination of uneducated people living in the wild and lonely, sometimes eerie surroundings" of the Highlands. However, the avalanche of Loch Ness Monster sightings began changing that notion. Maybe kelpies weren't just the daydreams of silly country folk. Maybe they were real!

Once again, the Nessie-kelpie connection was poorly made. The Loch Ness Monster didn't look like a horse, nor did it have adhesive skin. The only things they had in common were that they were mysterious lake dwellers in Scotland, and that the press seemed particularly fond of them.

Attempts to answer questions about the Loch Ness Monster ranged from rational to ludicrous. Fed up, a Scottish geologist named Henry Cadell wrote a silly poem about the whole debacle titled an "An Odious Ode to the Loch Ness Monster." It ran in the *Scotsman* in January, and made fun of the guessing game.

O Loch Ness Monster, who are you?
No kith or kin in any zoo.

Some prehistoric creature grim?
With feet and fins to walk and swim,
And den far down in some dark cave.
Fathoms unknown beneath the wave,
From which upon occasions rare
You sally up for change of air.
. . . are you sprung from ancient newts
That once were big and bony brutes
With swanlike necks (like Annie Laurie's)
And long nebb'd names like Plesiosauries?
Or from the northern kraken fell
The snake that ancient sages tell
Gobbled whole crews of Viking ships,
Then slipped o'erboard and smacked his lips? . . .
Plain folk who live beside Loch Ness
Describe the shape that you possess.
With neck and hump just like a camel
You're like a big aquatic mammal;
With horsey face and shaggy mane
You toss your head with proud disdain,
Your long tail sweeps like sculler's oar
And wavelets circle out to shore,
Then down mid swirling foam you dive.
No doubt you're very much alive. . . .
Mayhap you're one of a big brood
Residing here from babyhood.
But now you've come of age at last.
The whole world's eyes on you are cast.
Are you the remnant of your race
Deserving of an honoured place?

Much international attention
And at the last an old age pension?
Or else a monster to be dreaded,
Caught and shot and then beheaded?
This monstrous problem's to explore
And solve in 1934.

While some people spent their evenings arguing about which myths were based upon Nessie's ancient relatives and which theories made the most sense, skeptical scientists devoted their energy to exposing the forces behind the mania itself. Martin Hinton, the deputy keeper of zoology at the British Museum, didn't blame monster lovers for their enthusiasm. He said, "The observers, despite their good faith, appear to have been influenced subconsciously by three things, singly or in combination, namely, the Kelpie tradition, the sea-serpent myth, and by the picture postcards of the 'monster' on sale in Inverness."

While the world theorized about how, why, and when the Loch Ness Monster arrived in the lake, the pranksters behind the surgeon's photo were doing their best to steer clear of the Highland mystery altogether.

CHAPTER 17

RETREAT

Marmaduke Wetherell's photo ruse was a resounding success. The *Daily Mail* had bought it as a genuine article and printed it. People around the globe interpreted the *Mail*'s publication of the photo as proof that it was real. This would have been the perfect time for Wetherell to sabotage the *Daily Mail*. He could have burst forth, laughing, to announce the mortifying truth: it was all a joke! A whopper of a prank! The same paper that had ruined Wetherell's name for being a little overzealous, for telling one tiny white lie about a set of hippo footprints, was now the one who had pushed a lie onto its readership. It wasn't Wetherell who couldn't be trusted, but the *Daily Mail*! All Wetherell had to do was come clean about his prank. It would be so easy. Interestingly, Wetherell did no such thing.

Theories about why Wetherell kept his prank a secret vary. He might have chosen to remain quiet about his involvement to save face. In order to expose the *Daily Mail*'s journalistic blunder, someone would need to definitively discredit the surgeon's photo by explaining the prank. Part of laying the prank bare would involve revealing its players, too. Wetherell couldn't guarantee how that information would sit with the public. Would they find the involvement of his son, stepson, Maurice Chambers, and Dr. Wilson charming? Or would they find the whole ordeal distasteful? The prank had been so successful, the photo so widely believed that Wetherell couldn't guarantee how so many people would respond to learning they'd been fooled.

If the public turned on the men, the damage could be lasting. Wetherell knew better than anyone how something like that could impact a person's life and career. It would surely ding the reputation of Dr. Wilson, who had already been punished by the British Medical Association. The organization slapped his wrist and issued a £1,000 ($1,171) fine for allowing his name to be associated with the surgeon's photo, which was deemed an unfair advertising advantage over his peers. There was an underlying message in this fine, too: respectable doctors do not dabble in monster hunts. If Wilson had already faced such a reprimand for participating in a monster hunt that everyone thought was legitimate, he'd surely face much harsher consequences once everyone realized the photo was fake.

Wilson wouldn't be the only one at risk. What would happen to Wetherell's son, Ian? At the time of the surgeon's photo's release, Ian's career was on fire. In 1934 alone, he appeared in two plays at London's Hull Theatre, a 1,300-seat institution, and one at the Shaftesbury Theatre, which housed an impressive 1,400 velvety seats. His hard work and talent were earning him the attention he deserved. In addition to his stage work, he had four films coming out the next year. He was a handsome, talented, hardworking actor in the prime of his career. If the public learned the truth about his involvement in the hoax, his star might be quickly extinguished.

to snag the gig were dubbed "Watchers for the Monster" and driven to posts around the loch. To motivate his new crew, Mountain promised a bonus of ten guineas for each documented sighting. Unsurprisingly, tales of sightings poured in. Newspapers from Vancouver, Canada to Waterloo, Iowa reported on his progress, noting that Mountain's men logged more than twenty sightings and produced twenty-one photographs. The excitement soon fizzled, however, when the images were revealed. They were largely unimpressive, showing at best blurry dark objects, and at worst, the wake from passing boats. Mountain called it quits. Most of his watchers trudged back to the unemployment office, sure that their next job wouldn't be nearly as cushy or as bizarre.

One of Mountain's watchers wasn't quite ready to throw in the towel. Captain James Fraser kept a tent on the loch's northern shore and steadfastly continued to wait. On September 15, 1934, Fraser saw a dark object in the water. He remained impressively calm, thinking to himself, "I might as well shoot some film." He lifted his camera to his eye, "pressed the button" and congratulated himself when "fortunately it started to operate." Fraser nabbed about ten feet of film (roughly sixteen seconds' worth), then packed the precious evidence up and sent it straight off to Mountain in London for analysis. Mountain was thrilled at the development. He hurried to put together a luncheon for a group of London's top scientists at the swanky Waldorf Hotel. There, over the clatter of plates and tea saucers, the black-and-white film flickered to life. The audience squinted, then sighed. The film didn't show a monster. They determined that the creature Fraser had filmed was "probably a seal."

Once again, scientific experts had issued their verdict: there was no monster. And once again, enthusiastic monster fans and newspaper publishers inserted their fingers into their ears. In November 1934, Mountain tried again to convince the academic world that the monster was real by hosting a talk for the Linnean Society, a historic group of natural scientists. In his quest to bring these skeptics over to his side, Mountain used three tactics: a persuasive speech by Commander Gould, a rerun of Fraser's film, and, of course, a prominent display of the surgeon's photo.

Wetherell's prank, powered by an unchecked media, had spun entirely out of control. But the world's attention was about to shift. An entirely different kind of monster had begun creeping into the news.

CHAPTER 18

WAR

One week after the surgeon's photo first hit newsstands, a German tabloid called *Der Stürmer* greeted readers with a shocking image of its own. It was a black-and-white drawing that portrayed two machine cogs, each stamped with a swastika, slowly pulling a man between their teeth. The man is unshaven, with curly dark hair and an exaggeratedly large nose. He appears frantic. Sweat drips from his face. Stamped onto the machine cogs are words that translate to "Anyone who buys from a Jew is a traitor to the people. The Jews are our misfortune!"

Der Stürmer was a notoriously offensive paper. Its pages were filled with obscene images and rants against Jews, Catholics, and communists. It regularly depicted Jews as inferior, dangerous, and dirty. The paper's deliberately outrageous content was hard to stomach for plenty of Germans. At the time, it only sold about fifty thousand copies a week. In contrast, *Berliner Tageblatt*, a popular German newspaper, sold well over 130,000 copies each day. Despite its meager presence, *Der Stürmer* had one very monstrous supporter: Adolf Hitler. The short, foul-tempered Austrian had become Germany's chancellor in 1933, the same year the Loch Ness Monster made her grand debut.

At first, the two monsters were able to share the global supply of newsprint. One made headlines for her underwater theatrics, while the other dominated the press for his anti-Semitic policies. On July 22, 1933, the day of George Spicer's monster sighting, a British political group issued a call to action for "victims of the Hitler regime." It warned the world of something terribly frightening: "Concentration camps . . . crowded with victims . . . more harshly treated than prisoners of war." That wasn't all. It also reported that "[t]housands of others . . . forced under the menace of death, or worse" had fled to "seek refuge in the neighbouring countries." Things only escalated from there. On December 20, 1933, the day that Wetherell's "monster tracks" discovery published in the *Daily Mail*, another troubling story began circulating in the German press. A group of Nazi leaders had hatched an ambitious plan to "cleanse" the German population of impurities through forced sterilization. Anyone who they considered inferior would be made medically unable to have children. These updates were so frightening they seemed fit for a horror film. Unfortunately, they were all too real.

As Hitler's aggressions grew more audacious, they required more inches of newsprint. Around the same time, interest in the Loch Ness Monster waned. What had been a fun diversion— a monster in Scotland!—now felt terribly unimportant. Who had time to spend on Nessie when a far more menacing beast loomed just over the horizon in Germany? In August 1934, Hitler declared himself Germany's supreme leader, or führer. This political move ultimately set two trajectories: one which sent the world careening toward a global conflict and another that temporarily sank the Loch Ness Monster.

As months and then years ticked by, newspaper monster

mentions dropped significantly, reflecting either a drop in activity or a drop in reader interest. One reporter wondered if the monster "knew that it was unpatriotic to call attention to itself, and the loch it inhabits, while Britain was fighting for her life." In any case, the space previously devoted to meticulous descriptions of Nessie was now used to explain concepts such as *Volksgemeinschaft*, the racially unified German "people's community," and *lebensraum*, the increasing "living space" needed by the ever-growing German nation. It was a tectonic shift from the frivolous to the frightening.

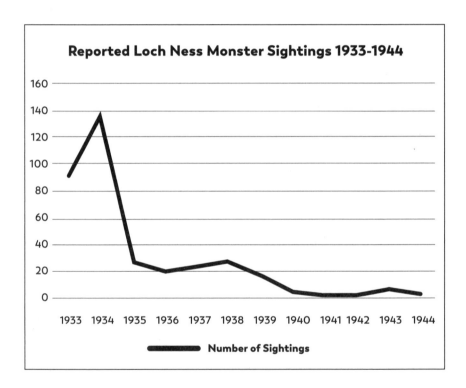

Hitler made a move toward getting more *lebensraum* by invading Czechoslovakia on March 15, 1939. The next morning, newspapers sounded the alarm at this troubling update. Headlines blared: "HITLER EXTENDS RULE" and "HERR HITLER ENTERS

PRAGUE." A second world war loomed. Mothers gazed at their sons with sickening fear. Would they be sent off to fight? Men eyed their homes and wondered—would their town be Hitler's next target? Life, security, and safety were no longer guaranteed. A German monster was on the move. Given this context, it is unsurprising that another news story that day received little attention.

It lay buried on page 4 of the *Kinematograph Weekly*, a publication aimed at people in the movie and theater worlds. "M. A. Wetherell has passed away in Johannesburg," the tiny article announced. It said that the actor and director would be "most warmly remembered." Wetherell had died of cancer while working on his final film, *Oom Paul*, which would never be completed. In his final years, Wetherell had managed to distance himself from the hippo-foot incident. Newspapers no longer linked him to the Loch Ness Monster. However, it might have been small consolation because newspapers had almost ceased to mention the filmmaker altogether. His name had mostly dropped from public awareness. The world was far too busy eyeing Herr Hitler's antics to pay attention to a former monster hunter.

World War II officially began on September 1, 1939. In an attempt to keep its armed forces fed and fueled, the UK began enforcing rations on food, fuel, and other resources. This, along with the fact that most able-bodied men were being called up to serve in the military, meant that Highland tourism was a vanishing trade. Loch Ness road traffic dwindled. Tour boats that had previously been overflowing with eager monster hunters now bobbed, empty and quiet, at their docks. Nessie postcards rustled in the wind at tourist kiosks.

Yet while Loch Ness Monster mania had finally cooled in the UK, it had only just begun to rankle enemy leadership abroad. Joseph Goebbels was especially annoyed. Goebbels was Germany's minister of propaganda. He headed a governmental group that strategically controlled and manipulated information in order to influence people. Under Hitler's direction, Goebbels used propaganda to convince millions of Germans that their actions were noble and necessary. He organized a campaign of movies, art, music, books, and more that reinforced this message. Part of Nazi Germany's propaganda involved rejecting independent newspapers and reporters who might report stories that conflicted with the official party line. Hitler had famously written that propaganda "must confine itself to a few points and repeat them over and over." To discredit non-Nazi newspapers and foreign reporters, Hitler's followers began repeating a label over and over. Independent publishers and journalists were the *Lügenpresse*, or lying press. Hitler's henchmen, who had made careers of printing false or manipulated information themselves, were slinging a deadly version of the schoolyard taunt: "I know you are, but what am I?"

When reports of the Loch Ness Monster made their way into Goebbels's luxurious summer home he sniffed in disdain. This Nessie had gone too far. She was obviously fake! A simple tourism hoax, designed to fool dopey Brits into wasting their money in Scotland. Goebbels's irritation grew. By 1940, he could take it no longer. The propaganda minister lashed out at the monster and her believers in the form of a two-page article for the German newspaper, *Hamburger Illustrierte*. In it, Goebbels asserted two things: Nessie wasn't real, and anyone stupid enough to believe in a loch monster would be easily vanquished by the intellectually superior Germans. These messages fit neatly into Goebbels's overall propaganda strategy, which boosted German confidence by knocking others down. But it also marked a significant milestone in Nessie's existence. She'd risen to such heights that a top Nazi was taking swings at her.

Later that year, apparently unsatisfied with his first assault on the monster, Goebbels gave it another try. This time, his propaganda team pushed a different message. They claimed that the Loch Ness Monster had been real but now it was dead. These Germans said that Nessie had bumped into an underwater mine, which detonated. The reports that followed this propaganda push were grim. A French radio host said that "pieces of its gigantic body have been washed ashore on the west coast of Scotland."

The next year, Italian journalists followed their German allies' lead and took a swipe of their own at Scotland's loch monster. Benito Mussolini's newspaper, *Il Popolo d'Italia*, reported that a warplane had bombed Nessie while on a raid through Scottish airspace. According to the paper, the airmen had looked down and seen the monster's corpse floating on the loch's surface. The Italians were attempting a propaganda strike of their own, claiming Scotland's beloved monster had been murdered. This was an effort to inflict emotional damage. Their story seemed legitimate. One American reporter noted, "this was the most convincing of all the reports, because the busy crew of a bombing plane, in the midst of their dangerous errand, would be the last persons in the world to imagine or invent a sea-serpent yarn."

Nessie lovers and profiteers weren't about to take this Italian assault sitting down. The *Daily Mail* responded by reporting on a fresh sighting by a Scotsman named Mr. J. MacFarland-Barrow. The article reassured a whole nation of readers that the monster appeared to be "in really high spirits." The *Mail* laid it on thick: "How could MacFarland-Barrow have seen the monster," it asked, "When *Popolo d'Italia* knows it has been killed?" With this rhetorical question, the *Mail* both informed its readership of Nessie's health and insulted the Italians.

The fake assassination by the Italians soon became a metaphor for British wartime resiliency. "Possibly scarred and even shell-shocked," one reporter wrote, the monster was "outwardly as good as ever." They went on, explaining that Nessie "may be a monster," but she had "some sturdy, bull-dog characteristics which the British admire." The reporter noted that the monster "took a whole stick of bombs but is back, doing business at the same old stand, just as people do in London and Coventry." The bogus Italian news story hadn't just failed to extinguish Nessie; it had actually elevated her. Now, the monster was being discussed as though it were a bloodied infantryman, marching across the battlefield. Nessie wasn't just a lake monster anymore. She was an inspiration for hundreds of thousands of browbeaten Allied soldiers.

One such soldier was familiar to the players in the photo hoax: R. K. Wilson. Though known in the newspapers as the "London surgeon," Wilson identified less as a doctor and more as a soldier. He'd fought valiantly in World War I, then spent the 1930s nurturing an interest in firearms and warfare and telling anyone who would listen that another war was coming. When his predictions came true and WWII broke out, Wilson leapt at his chance to resume his soldier's life. But rather than reenacting his WWI exploits in the Royal Artillery, Wilson wound up in the Special Operations Executive. This branch of the British armed forces dealt in secrets and trickery—two things with which Wilson had plenty of experience. Wilson became a pioneering operative in Operation Jedburgh, a secret program that worked with Dutch resistance groups to fight German forces in occupied Holland and France. Operation Jedburgh required its operatives to quite literally drop into their field positions. In Wilson's case, this meant jumping out of airplanes and hoping the enemy didn't shoot him on his way down. Wilson lucked out. The Germans never caught him, and his efforts earned him a Croix de Guerre from France and the Order of Orange-Nassau from the Netherlands. Some Londoners might have been surprised to learn that their friendly neighborhood physician was, in fact, a talented spy. But, as he had shown during the surgeon's photo hoax, Wilson was a talented con man. He fit right into the world of espionage.

World War II also impacted another conspirator behind the surgeon's photo. Christian Spurling moved to Malaysia in 1937 to work on a tea and rubber plantation. Japanese forces took him prisoner in 1942 and shuttled him between various POW camps until the war ended in 1945. It was a grueling ordeal for the model maker. He lost nearly one hundred pounds over his three-year captivity, and endured terrible discomfort and stress. To cope with the torment, Spurling and his fellow prisoners told stories to pass the time. Spurling, perhaps inspired by his years helping on his stepfather's film sets, saw his chance to step into the spotlight. He broke his silence about the surgeon's photo, giving something of a lecture about the whole plot. His fellow prisoners listened eagerly as he unspooled the terrific tale. *The Loch Ness Monster photo was a fake!* Spurling later recalled his performance. "Interesting," he said dryly, the story sure "kept the boys interested."

Perhaps even more interesting, however, is the fact that none of Spurling's fellow POWs shared his confession after they returned home. This might have been because they forgot about it or because they didn't believe it in the first place. Or maybe they were simply too relieved to have survived their captivity to want to relive any of its details, even something as extraordinary as the prank of the century. In any case, Spurling's secret was safe. No one publicized the truth about the surgeon's photo. The hoax lived on.

CHAPTER 19

FLIPPERS

On August 8, 1972, a crescent moon glowed in the summer sky. Below it, a small cluster of boats bobbed peacefully on the ink black surface of Loch Ness. Huddled inside their cabins were members of a state-of-the-art monster hunt, led by Robert Rines, an esteemed Massachusetts Institute of Technology professor and president of the Academy of Applied Sciences.

Rines, fifty, didn't look like a stuffy academic. He had an easy smile and naturally curly hair that occasionally hovered around his head like the fluff on a dandelion. All night, Rines and his crew had been monitoring the feedback from a sonar device they'd lowered from their boat, *Narwhal*, to the loch's floor. Small dark spots flitted across the sonar feed. Rines knew they were just fish in search of midnight snacks. Still, hope remained that something larger might appear at any moment. In case that should occur, the monster hunters had also lowered a special camera from another vessel, *Nan*. This camera had been programmed to snap photos at timed intervals at the same moment that a powerful flash flared. If everything went according to plan, the flash would illuminate the murky water right as the camera snapped *and* as the sonar collected readings, giving researchers a multipronged collection of data. They wouldn't just get photographic evidence; they'd also get sonar echo-sound results. These would confirm that something real had passed in front of the lens. The camera held two thousand frames of film.

During the previous two decades, monster hunters had tried all sorts of tricks in order to spot, study, or even capture Nessie. There was the autogiro pilot, who'd launched a monthlong aerial hunt. There was the team who'd beamed superpowered spotlights across the loch's surface each night, hoping to catch the monster on a midnight prowl. There were expeditions mounted by respected academic institutions, such as Harvard and Cambridge, and haphazard, single-person monster hunts. An official-sounding organization called the Loch Ness Investigation Bureau formed, mounted organized searches, and cataloged information. Between 1963 and 1972, the bureau logged a hearty two hundred eyewitness accounts of the monster.

In the face of all these sightings and all this work, hard evidence of Nessie's existence remained elusive. The surgeon's photo and a handful of other blurry, indistinct images were all that the loch had offered in the previous thirty-nine years. Science demanded more. Hunters deployed hydrophones, still cameras, video cameras, submarines, and sonar scanners, all in an attempt to satisfy this demand. So far, everyone had come up short.

Rines hoped to give the world new proof that Nessie was real. Back in 1970, he'd cruised around the loch, trailing a drum of freeze-dried salmon oils and other strong-smelling fish products. He hoped these substances might lure Nessie close enough for him to observe the creature. While Rines didn't manage to spot the beast on this trip, he did get a few interesting sonar readings that suggested a large animal had swum beneath him. These spurred him on. The following year, he returned to the loch to continue hunting. He did more sonar sweeps and spotted a "twenty-foot-long hump" moving across the water. "This," Rines later said, "destroyed any last doubts I had that we are dealing with a very large living creature here at Loch Ness."

On that dark summer night in 1972, it looked like Rines was about to destroy the world's doubts about Nessie, too. At about 1:40 a.m., salmon began to break the loch's surface with frantic movement. Rines's crew immediately checked their sonar. Something strange was happening. The sonar showed that the area's fish were disappearing, almost as if they were evading a predator. "Then it started," a crew member would later recall. Five minutes after the fish fled, "a big, black trace started to appear" on the sonar. "To begin with we thought it must be two or three fish close together. But then it got bigger and blacker and thicker; we could hardly believe our eyes–something huge was moving down there." Below them, the camera flashed and the sonar scanned.

As soon as the sun came up, Rines's team collected their sonar data, reeled in their underwater equipment, and made for shore. They carefully extracted the film from the camera and days later hand delivered it to Kodak's headquarters in New York. There, employees were made to sign statements affirming that the film had not been tampered with before they could begin processing it. Their results revealed that between 1:45 a.m. and 1:55 a.m., at precisely the time his sonar had recorded the huge mystery object, Rines's camera had captured four strange images. They were terribly blurry, but appeared to reveal a subject of some sort gliding past the lens. Was it the monster? The sediment and haze in the image made it too hard to know for sure.

Rines promptly sent the images off for photo enhancement at NASA's Jet Propulsion Laboratory in California. This facility had previously enhanced photographs from space missions and was well equipped for the task. A PhD student and technician there named Alan Gillespie got right to work. Using his own image-enhancing technique, he scanned the images into a digital format and fed them into a computer program that used filters to make the images crisper. Next, he converted the computer data back into film. It was a tricky, meticulous process. But by the time he'd finished, Gillespie suspected that the photos did indeed show something. He just didn't know what that something was.

Gillespie returned the enhanced images to Rines. Shortly after, Rines shared two of the images with editors at *Time* magazine and a few other newspapers, who snatched them up for publication. The photos hit newsstands in November and made an immediate splash. The images that Gillespie hadn't been able to decipher now very clearly showed a monster's huge flippers, as though the beast had glided right past one of the submerged cameras. The detail was stunning. The flippers were diamond-shaped, with a long central ridge. They tapered slightly before connecting to a knobby, barrel-shaped torso. Readers around the world gaped in awe. Alan Gillespie stared in alarm. These were not the images he'd passed on to Rines. Lines had been sharpened; shadows had been darkened. Someone had clearly altered the images.

Analysis of the corresponding sonar data added a disappointing layer to the story. It turned out that neither Rines's sonar device nor camera had been fixed in place underwater. They had instead been lowered on tethers that allowed them to move somewhat

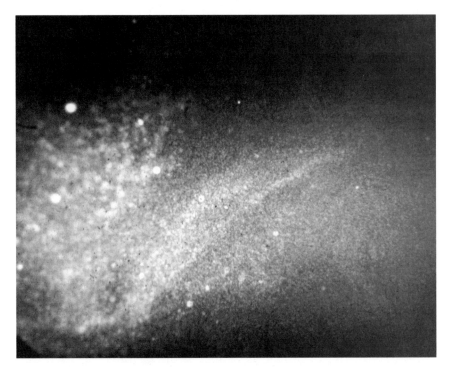

Robert Rines's original "Flipper" photo

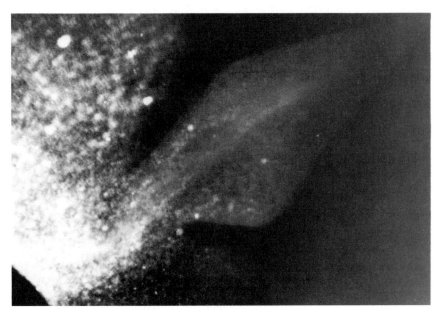

Robert Rines's "Flipper" photo after enhancement

freely on the water currents. The camera and sonar device could have been pointed up, down, or sideways. This made their findings unreliable. Researchers couldn't tell which sonar readings reflected an object moving past and which simply showed the device wobbling over the floor of the loch.

Though scientists learned about the issues with Rines's work shortly after the "flipper" photos went public, most of their concerns didn't make it into the press. Even when a former employee of the British Museum complained that "Rines, presumably, is so stupid that he doesn't know when his camera is operating in mid-water and when it is sitting on the bottom," the media didn't latch onto this narrative. This allowed the public to go on thinking that Rines's groundbreaking photos were, at the very least, plausible.

Much as the surgeon's photo had done in the 1930s, Rines's photos started a newspaper domino effect in which editors at papers all around the world felt compelled to share the stunning images with their readers. Rines's photos were splashed across papers from Australia to Canada under headlines like "Scientists Photograph Ness Monster" and "The Loch Ness Monster is Alive and Well." Many of these images accompanied articles that recalled the original 1930s narrative: there was a monster in Loch Ness after all! Some went even farther, declaring that there were *two* monsters in the loch. Others took a more neutral stance. An Associated Press story reminded its readers that the monster was "still unexplained." The photos, while thrilling, remained "inconclusive." A Florida paper went further: "O What Could It Be . . . The Famed Loch Nessie?" Its headline waffled before answering its own question: "Maybe."

In 1975, Rines returned to the loch and delivered more

evidence to sway the naysayers. On this mission, he again used high-tech underwater photography. Again, he succeeded. This time he walked away with two more images of the monster. One photo appeared to show its bulbous body and long, curving neck. The other image showed a frightening close-up of the gnarled head of a gargoyle-like plesiosaur. Its mouth hung open as if caught in a silent bellow. Together with his previous photographs, called the flipper pictures, these became known as the "whole body" and the "gargoyle." Rines celebrated his new images by partnering with Sir Peter Scott, a famed naturalist. The pair co-authored an article in one of the world's most respected scientific journals, *Nature*, about the monster. This article also finally bestowed Nessie with a real, authentic, scientific name. From then on, she would be known as *Nessiteras rhombopteryx*, Latin for "Ness monster with diamond-shaped fin." In addition to giving the creature an official name, Rines gave the world a clear picture of her appearance. She was a large, barrel-chested, flippered creature with a long, narrow neck and small head. In short, she looked quite a bit like the creature in the surgeon's photo.

Whether intentionally or not, Rines was operating within a framework established by Marmaduke Wetherell back in 1934. Wetherell's creature was plesiosaur-like, with a long head and small neck. Though not visible in the photo, most people presumed that the creature in the surgeon's photo had flippers. The photographic evidence that Rines collected—showing flippers, head, and full body—all fit Wetherell's monster model. Rines wasn't the only monster hunter who found his work echoing the surgeon's photo. Over and over again, eyewitnesses recounted seeing a creature that looked just like Wetherell's fake. They described its "serpent-like head," and "elongated and slim" neck which rose gracefully over the water. It was as if Wetherell had written a script for monster hunters, and the *Mail* had passed it out to the world. Anyone who wanted their sighting to be believed had to stick to it.

As the years passed, all of Rines's photos were discredited. The flipper photos were exposed as having been heavily manipulated, though the identity of the manipulator was never discovered. And the gargoyle and whole body images were revealed to show underwater debris. The whole body is likely just a stick, and the gargoyle is a lumpy tree stump that was identified in 1987. Thus, the most scientifically recognized modern images of the Loch Ness Monster fell into the surgeon's photo's well-worn shadow. They were baloney, and they sold a lot of newspapers.

CHAPTER 20

TRUTH

On a chill, December day in 1975, a gray-haired Ian Wetherell stood behind the glossy wooden bar of his London pub, the Cross Keys. Above its doors hung a pair of enormous wooden keys. These were a nod to the historic practice that helped illiterate patrons find their desired drinking locations and an interesting irony. Wetherell held the keys to the world's greatest monster hoax. After forty-one years of secrecy, the former actor was ready to unlock the truth.

A reporter from the *Sunday Telegraph* walked under the keys and into the pub. Wetherell began, "My father, Marmaduke Wetherell, was a fairly well-known big-game hunter," his voice ringing out with its clear, upper-crust accent. "The *Mail* commissioned him to look for the monster. . . . When he reported— as he had expected—that there were no signs of life, [editors at the *Mail*] seemed rather peeved. So my father said, 'All right, we'll give them their monster.'" Wetherell continued, telling the reporter about getting the camera and about how they'd crafted the monster: "We made it from one of the little toy submarines you could buy for about half-a-crown, plus some rubber tubing and what-have-you. It was only a few inches high." He went on, describing how they found the perfect setting for the image and how they'd sent the toy floating out onto the water. "It was just a matter of winding up the sub and getting it to dive just below the surface so the neck and head drew a proper little V in the water." Finally, he confessed to taking "about five" photos of the toy beast, one of which went on to become the famed Surgeon's Photo.

Wetherell's detailed admission was groundbreaking. It also occurred during a very busy, chaotic period in London's history. In the months leading up to Wetherell's meeting with the reporter, waves of Irish Republican Army (IRA) gun violence and bombings had destabilized the city. Restaurants, hotels, and residences had been attacked as part of the IRA's campaign to bully the British into pulling their troops out of Northern Ireland. Terror reigned. The violence reached a climax the night before Wetherell's confession appeared in the *Sunday Telegraph*, when a group of IRA gunmen fired bullets into a ritzy London restaurant. Police pursued, and the IRA men tore through the city on a high-speed car chase, firing on law enforcement. The gunmen burst into a small basement apartment and took the residents hostage. The following morning, Londoners bit their nails as they digested the news. People weren't safe anywhere anymore, not even in their own homes! The IRA hostage crisis was all anyone could talk about. It completely overshadowed everything else, including a fascinating *Sunday Telegraph* article titled "Making of a Monster," in which the Loch Ness Monster photo hoax was revealed.

Wetherell's confession *should* have been headline news around the world. The *Sunday Telegraph* sold about 759,000 copies each week. That meant that 759,000 people *should* have been rushing to their telephones to spread the word. But none of that happened because at the precise moment that Wetherell's admission hit newsstands, London was descending into utter turmoil. Many newspaper readers didn't have the time or energy to spend digging into the details of a decades-old photograph. They were busy stepping over broken glass and bullet shells. Similarly, editors at rival newspapers probably saw the confession and shrugged, opting not to run the story in their own papers. And thus, the confession of the century evaporated like morning mist over a summer loch.

Ian Wetherell's confession, printed in the *Sunday Telegraph* on December 7, 1975.

Making of a monster

NOW that we may not shortly see those underwater Loch Ness photographs, the man who took the most famous Loch Ness monster picture of all time comes clean at last: it was a fake.

Back in 1934 the *Daily Mail* astonished the world with the picture scoop of the century— a half-page giant, plus some smaller supporting shots, showing a long reptilian neck and little head, unmistakably forging through the waves on the loch. In the distance were the familiar shoreline and mountains. The caption gave the exact time and place.

Alas, there were no further sightings, and some scientists were unsporting enough to suggest that this particular Nessie wasn't palaeontologically very convincing. The *Mail* let the subject subside, so to speak.

Mandrake tracked down Ian Wetherell, now 63, behind the bar of the Cross Keys pub in Chelsea, where he has been landlord since the early 'Fifties. In 1934 he had been a young actor.

"The Loch Ness monster was one of the great silly season standbys at that time," he said. "My father, Marmaduke Wetherell, was a fairly well-known big-game hunter. The *Mail* commissioned him to look for the monster, using Asdic

equipment and so on. When he reported—as he had expected— that there were no signs of life, they seemed rather peeved.

"So my father said, 'All right, we'll give them their monster.' I remember that we drove up to Scotland again in his Hillman. There was a friend of his called Chambers, an insurance broker— they're both dead now. I had the camera, which was a Leica, and still rather a novelty then.

"Chambers had a shoot on one side of the Loch. He was the one who sent off the pictures—actually the undeveloped strip of film, saying he'd seen the creature while out shooting and tried to snap it. In fact we made it from one of the little toy submarines you could buy for about half-a-crown, plus some rubber tubing and what-have-you. It was only a few inches high.

"We found an inlet where the tiny ripples would look like full size waves out on the loch, and with the actual scenery in the background. Then it was just a matter of winding up the sub and getting it to dive just below the surface so the neck and head drew a proper little V in the water.

"I took about five shots with the Leica, then suddenly a water bailiff turned up. I suppose he had heard voices and thought we were fishing. Dad put his foot on the monster and sank it, and that was that."

In the years that followed, belief in the Loch Ness Monster persisted, despite Wetherell's admission and mounting evidence to the contrary. Dozens of researchers from multiple countries scanned, probed, and tested Loch Ness, coming up with precisely zilch to support the idea that a giant monster lurked in its depths. In 1987, Operation Deepscan used twenty boats to complete a total sonar scan of the loch and still failed to find Nessie. In the 1990s, a study of eyewitness testimony was conducted. In it, test administrators raised and lowered a wooden pole in Loch Ness in front of test subjects who were asked to draw what they saw. Researchers called about two-thirds of respondents' sketches "fairly accurate," while the remaining third got creative, drawing periscopes, knobs, and, in one case, a duck. This study emphasized the unreliable nature of eyewitness testimony, calling into question the hundreds of monster sightings on Loch Ness. The evidence against Nessie piled up.

Despite this, affection for Nessie only seemed to grow. Tributes to the Loch Ness Monster popped up everywhere. In 1978, Busch Gardens in Williamsburg, Virginia, debuted its Loch Ness Monster, a banana yellow, 3,240-foot, double-looping steel roller coaster. Film and television featured very different characterizations of the monster, from Disney's chipper *Nessie* in 1974 to the cheesy 1981 thriller, *The Loch Ness Horror*. Nessie starred in several genres of literature, including children's books, science fiction, and the monster-focused cryptofiction. Nessie fans ranged from children to grandparents, from scientists to politicians. A few celebrities even got in on the fun. Two members of the rock band AC/DC spent a cold, wet night trying to lure the monster with some unconventional bait: a box of fireworks. The pair thought that the monster might be attracted by their pyrotechnics. Unfortunately for them, Nessie didn't show. Actor Charlie Sheen went on a monster hunt of his own in 2013. While floating on the lake in a rowboat, he claimed to have spotted "an event at the top of the water that was crazy."

In the late 1980s and early 1990s, a pair of researchers named Alastair Boyd and David Martin got in on the action. They began rifling through a few Loch Ness Monster hunters' collections of old newspaper articles and letters. There, they stumbled upon Ian Wetherell's "Making of a Monster" article. It had apparently been filed but not understood. They also found other evidence backing up Wetherell's claims, including correspondence from a man who said that Wilson had once "quietly" confessed that he had "hoaxed the local inhabitants of Loch Ness." Wanting to know more, Boyd and Martin tried to find Ian Wetherell. They discovered that he had died, but that he had a stepbrother named Christian Spurling, an artist and model maker. The researchers traveled to Spurling's home in Southern England and were welcomed by a white-haired octogenarian who wasted no time in telling them the truth about the surgeon's photo: "It's not a genuine photograph. It's a load of codswallop and always has been."

Martin and Boyd went on, tracking down evidence to support Spurling's confession. They found a hippo-foot ashtray, quite similar to what Marmaduke Wetherell would have used, among his son Ian's belongings. Convinced, the pair decided to share the news with the world. On March 13, 1994, almost exactly six decades after the surgeon's photo first printed, their story appeared on the front page of the *Sunday Telegraph*. The headline said it all: "Revealed: Loch Ness Picture Hoax. Monster Was a Toy Submarine."

Other news outlets rushed to carry the story and cash in on the renewed interest. The *Daily Mail*, the paper that started it all, ran the surgeon's photo again. This time it appeared under the headline, "MOCK NESS MONSTER." Finally, the truth about the surgeon's photo made it ito the press. It was the end of an era. Or it should have been.

CHAPTER 21

TODAY

The truth about the surgeon's photo might have extinguished belief in the Loch Ness Monster for good. The photograph had spent sixty years as the linchpin in countless monster hunters' arguments. It was the evidence they pointed to when all else failed. The *New York Times* even called it one of the "most powerful arguments [. . .] that Nessie exists." When David Martin and Alastair Boyd went public with their discovery—that the surgeon's photo was actually a hoax—they robbed the world of one the most potent and recognizable pieces of Loch Ness Monster proof. And yet, belief in the monster did not fizzle out.

A recent study showed that about one in every four Scots believe in the Loch Ness Monster. In America, the numbers are slightly lower, with about 18 percent of survey participants reporting that Nessie is real. The English bring up the rear, with about 17 percent replying that they believe in the Loch Ness Monster. In August 2023, hundreds of hopeful cryptid fans descended upon Loch Ness in largest organized monster hunt in decades. Though the hunt was unsuccessful, participants' enthusiasm prompted an important question: how, in the face of modern science and the truth about the surgeon's photo, can such belief remain?

Loch Ness Monster researcher, Ronald Binns, has a guess. He thinks that confirmation bias, the tendency to search for and focus on things that support what you already believe, is to blame for much modern monster belief: "Monster experts tend to be enthusiastic amateurs, seeking evidence which reinforces a belief already held, not disinterested enquirers after the truth." Confirmation bias taints research. People looking to strengthen their existing theories are not open to contradictions or new information. They limit their searches and set their radars to only the frequencies they're interested in. Confirmation bias can inspire Bigfoot fans to read article after article about Bigfoot sightings, while avoiding articles that explain how many Bigfoot sightings are usually just tree stumps or bears.

Expectant attention might also be at play. This is the name for a phenomenon in which a person is so primed to see something that their brains trick them into thinking they've seen it, even when it's not there at all. Expectant attention can happen when people are extremely interested, curious, or motivated to spot something in particular. A relevant example of expectant attention comes from Tasmania. There, people have developed a strong sense of pride and interest in an animal known as the Tasmanian tiger. This oddball marsupial, which looked like a mash-up between a kangaroo, coyote, and tiger, went extinct in 1936. In the years since, however, curiosity about the tiger has only grown. Locals, sipping from aluminum cans decorated with Tasmanian tigers and driving cars with Tasmanian tiger license plates, stare into the bush and wonder: is it really gone? Some optimistic Tasmanians don't think so. Between 2016 and 2020, there were eight reported Tasmanian tiger sightings. Scientists have thus far explained them all away as misidentified animals, hoaxes, or as incidents of expectant attention. People just really wanted to see tigers. Likewise, many Nessie sightings can probably be explained away in a similar fashion. People just really want to see the old girl.

Others have suggested a different explanation for the lingering belief in Nessie: pareidolia. This is a psychological phenomenon in which a person perceives patterns or shapes that do not exist. In 1976, NASA unintentionally gave the world a lesson in pareidolia when its Viking 1 spacecraft captured an image from the surface of Mars. Now known as the "Face on Mars," the picture appeared to show a huge, ghastly human face rising out of the planet. It had two eyes, a nose, and a grimacing mouth. It was terrifying, and sent people into waves of panic. Was it proof of life on Mars? An alien artifact? NASA scientists rushed to

The "Face on Mars," which is actually just an oddly shaped mesa.

reassure the public that it just showed a landform that happened to look like a face, but some remained skeptical. It wasn't until 1998, when the space agency captured a higher resolution image, that the issue was put to bed. It wasn't a face. It was just an oddly shaped mesa. As with the "Face on Mars," people who believe they have seen the Loch Ness Monster may also have experienced pareidolia. Their brains took in the shape of a stick, wave, or sea otter and interpreted it as a monster.

A psychological concept known as homophily may also contribute to continued belief in Nessie. This is the name for the way people tend to spend time with others who share their views. Homophily is well summed up in the idiom, "birds of a feather flock together." In the case of the Loch Ness Monster, this can be seen in the way that Nessie fans tend to be drawn to other Nessie fans. This attraction creates social circles in which belief in monsters is normalized or even expected. Homophily can lead to an echo chamber of monster talk in which different parties repeat the same messages.

Likewise, there may be a reactive social component at play, too. Nessie believers—and cryptozoologists in general—often struggle for acceptance in modern scientific communities. They are rejected for their beliefs or for practicing "pseudoscience." Academics, who have spent their careers in research libraries, poring over peer-reviewed data, and dutifully climbing the established ladder toward professional recognition, sometimes see monster hunters as biased, uneducated, or undisciplined. But rather than weakening cryptozoology communities, this disdain actually often strengthens them. Cryptid fans have turned academia's rejection on its head and embraced their reputation as oddballs. Monster blogs and message boards give cryptid fans an online gathering place where they can meet, mingle, and befriend like-minded people. In-person, monster-themed conferences, such as CryptidCon, proudly cater to "legend trippers, crypto-enthusiasts, and all other fellow weirdos." There, people can bond by sharing monster legends, photographs, and theories. In this way, belief in cryptids such as the Loch Ness Monster can become a portal to social connectivity and friendship, a powerful motivator.

Another explanation for continued belief in the Loch Ness Monster actually has nothing to do with the monster at all. People believe in Nessie because of what it means about the rest of the universe. A world in which Nessie is real is a world in which time travel, flying cars, and telekinesis could also be real. As Dr. June Singer, a psychotherapist, put it, "We need the Loch Ness monster the same way we need to make trips to the moon—to go beyond the known to what people have never before seen." Adrian Shine, author and well-known Loch Ness investigator, echoes this. "As the human world shrinks, people tend to look for something bigger than themselves—something frightening, something mysterious or something hidden."

This desire to believe in the Loch Ness Monster is wildly contagious, even among skeptics. Some nonbelievers feel jealous of Nessie's ardent fans. To them, the world of Nessie believers is one of fun, excitement, possibility, and adventure. Former UK Prime Minister, Boris Johnson, said in 2019, "There is a part of my soul that still yearns to believe [in the Loch Ness Monster]." Betty Macdougall, the former curator of the Loch Ness Monster Exhibition, put it another way, "I don't want *not* to believe."

Without a doubt, exaggerated, inaccurate reporting and media-fueled misinformation bear the most responsibility for belief in a mythical lake monster. Beginning in the 1930s, when the idea of a loch beast first emerged, publishers pedaled unreliable, error-filled, and sensational stories to a public hungry for them. They fudged quotes, omitted contradictory information, and formatted their stories in order to provide the most astonishing, gotta-buy-it content possible. In this way, 1930s media created a foundation of belief in Nessie. Over the following decades, these beliefs solidified. Today, mainstream, respected publishers no longer print wildly false Nessie stories. But plenty of unreliable sources, such as blogs and tabloids, still do. In 2009 the *National Enquirer* declared "Loch Ness Monster Found." In 2021, a headline in the *Globe* screamed "Loch Ness Monster Caught on Camera!" These publications use scandalous headlines and misleading text to fool their readers.

Social media, too, plays a huge role in the spread of misinformation about Nessie. As of 2024, TikTok videos with the hashtag #lochnessmonster had more than 300 million views. #Nessie was even more impressive, with 659 million views. This shows the power and reach of sensational media. It also shows that belief in Nessie isn't going away anytime soon.

While some people bemoan Nessie's staying power, others don't mind at all. A 2018 study found that Loch Ness Monster tourism adds roughly £41 million ($48 million) a year to Scotland's economy. Tourism ambassador and director of Loch Ness Marketing, Willie Cameron, thinks the numbers are probably higher than that. He also says, "At the end of the day, I suppose that it doesn't really matter if you believe whether the monster exists or not as she's working for the whole of Scotland anyway."

Born of an unchecked media and elevated by a disgruntled

actor's hoax, the Loch Ness Monster has transformed into an icon of hope, mystery, and possibility. She has inspired generations of children to look closely at the world around them, yet she also serves as a cautionary tale about the dangers of misinformation in the news. Considering all this, it is sometimes difficult to know how to think about Nessie and her surrounding mythology. Is she just a silly story? The outcome of a runaway hoax? A byproduct of 1930s science and art? Perhaps it is best to think of the Loch Ness Monster the same way Marmaduke Wetherell thought of his prank all those years ago: with a wink.

CHAPTER 22

TIPS

The story of the Loch Ness Monster myth might seem at first to be a quaint, historical tale of unruly reporters and their gullible, old-timey readers. However, it's actually a great example of a phenomenon that continues to plague modern media: fake news.

Fake news is the name for media stories that are false or deliberately misleading. It occupies a blurry spot in modern vocabularies, sitting somewhere between or on top of misinformation and disinformation. (Misinformation is false or misleading information that is shared, regardless of intent. Disinformation is false or misleading information that is *purposefully* shared.) And though the term fake news gained popularity in the 2016 American presidential election, it is actually a centuries-old issue. It was a part of the French Revolution and a part of the American Revolutionary War. In 1835, an American fake news story caused thousands of people to believe that the moon was teeming with alien life. Sixty years later, another fake news story caused such a ruckus that it contributed to the outbreak of the Spanish-American War. For as long as fake news has existed, people have been annoyed about it. American Founding Father, Thomas

Jefferson, once said, "Nothing can now be believed which is seen in a newspaper."

Today, fake news continues to contribute to all sorts of social, political, and cultural events. It is the force behind a rising distrust in government and science. It has also become a negative label. People who do not like a particular news story may try to discredit it by calling it fake news. Some modern fake news comes from media companies. These organizations might use fake news to sway their readers' opinions about politics. Other fake news comes from foreign governments who are also looking to shift public opinion about political leaders. Some fake news is generated at home by individuals. Regardless of the source, these stories can have monumental impacts.

Confronting fake news requires media literacy. This is an umbrella term for a set of critical thinking skills used to analyze, evaluate, and critique what appears in the news media. It also refers to the way that people handle the news—whether they ignore it, use it, or share it. If people in the 1930s were more media literate, it is very likely that the story of the Loch Ness Monster would have fizzled out quickly. People would have recognized it as fake news and dismissed it. While a world without Nessie is slightly sad to imagine, a world without fake news seems downright delightful.

Media literacy requires vigilance. Being media literate means seeing the world through a skeptical and analytical filter at all times, whether when reading a newspaper or when scrolling through X (formerly known as Twitter). It means asking critical questions and thinking hard about who is behind every message. Media literate people must constantly wade through the soup of spin, bias, and misinformation. But these efforts are well worth the work.

You can do your part to identify fake news by becoming media literate. Check out the following media literacy tips and try to use them the next time you find yourself reading a news story. You might be surprised at what you discover.

1. CHECK THE HEADLINE

The first thing you should do when assessing news media is look at the headline. Is it straightforward, like "Scientists Identify New Fish in Loch Ness" or is it provocative or sensational, like "Is a Nightmare Lurking in Loch Ness? Click Here to Find Out!" If the headline seems designed to provoke fear, anger, or another strong emotion, you may be dealing with fake news.

CLICKBAIT

Clickbait is online content that is designed specifically to catch attention so that users click on it and generate money from site advertisers. Headlines and photos are often deliberately misleading and enticing, like "Girl Walks into Pet Shop. You Won't Believe What Happens Next!" or "Tips to Get Stronger While You Sleep. Number 4 Will Blow Your Mind!" Be very careful when you see clickbait headlines. The stories below may be full of fake news or misinformation.

2. WHO PUBLISHED IT?

The next thing to look at when considering news is the website or publisher. Is it a reliable source, such as the *Wall Street Journal* or *New York Times*, or is it *UnbelievableNews4You.net*? Traditional news media companies employ trained journalists and editors who work to ensure that their content is accurate through diligent research and fact-checking. Sensational or satirical publishers do not. If you're considering news from an online site, you'll need to be extra thorough. Check the URL. Many fake news sites use URLs that closely resemble the URLs of legitimate news sources with just a few letters changed. If you still aren't sure, click on the news site's "contact us" or "about" page. There, you should be able to tell if the site is a traditional news site, or if it includes fake or joke content.

SATIRE

Some websites feature satire or humor. *The Onion* is a popular satirical news publisher. It runs silly stories that often relate loosely to current events. Sometimes people see *Onion* headlines and believe they are reading a real news story. In 2009, the *Onion* ran a story about Apollo 11 astronaut, Neil Armstrong, realizing that he "did not in fact travel 250,000 miles over eight days" and "touch down on the moon," but had instead been fooled into participating in a moon hoax. Not realizing that the *Onion* article was a joke, editors at a Bangladeshi news outlet called the *Daily Manab Zamin* reported on the story as though it was true. The paper later issued an apology: "We are sorry for publishing the report without checking the information."

3. WHO WROTE IT?

You're still not done vetting your source. Now, check out who wrote the article. Most news sites will not only list the author but will also provide a link to their biography, website, or X feed. Click through to see who they are, how they are qualified to write about the topic, and what else they've written. If their bio sounds too good to be true, like "John Monster has caught four sea serpents, holds three Olympic long-distance swimming gold medals, and likes to bake croissants in his spare time," it probably isn't real. If the author is a journalist who has published other work on the same subject matter on reliable sites, they're probably a good source.

BIAS

Some news stories are reported in a biased way. This means they take one side of an issue rather than reporting on both sides equally. Bias can appear through a writer's tone or in the way a reporter spins a story. It can also appear in the way a news outlet treats the article. Editors may choose to feature it on the front page of a paper or bury it in the back pages. Stories that take up space on a website's homepage or on the front page seem more important than those hidden elsewhere.

Bias is impossible to remove entirely. However, quality news sources should strive to avoid as much bias as possible. This means they should work to present both sides of a story, to cite a variety of sources, and to utilize reporters and journalists who will work to publish fair, balanced news.

Readers, too, should do their best to become aware of their own biases and to consume media from a variety of sources. When readers only get their news from people who share their same biases, they can fall into the trap of living inside "echo chambers." This means that they say and hear the same things over and over, in an endless cycle of agreeing and repeating. Experts have pointed to the "echo chamber" news consumption habit as a key factor behind the "us versus them" mentality that can develop between people who disagree.

4. CHECK THE QUOTES

If the article includes quotations, take a peek at who gave them. Google their names. Are they well-known experts on the subject? Or does the article quote a celebrity who decided to weigh in? If the source is not named, this can be a red flag. Journalists usually name their sources unless doing so will put the sources in danger or cause them harm.

5. CHECK THE IMAGE

Many online articles include photographs. Reliable news articles will feature photo credits. These usually appear in light text below the photo and include the name of the photographer or photo agency. If there is no photo credit, this might be a sign that you're reading content from an unreliable site. Do a reverse image search. This will show you the original source of the image which can help you decide if the article you're reading is trustworthy.

6. ONLINE CHECK

If you've done all of the above and you're still not sure, don't worry. There are websites out there that exist to help you with this exact scenario. Snopes, FactCheck.org, and others are constantly updating their sites to alert users of trending fake news stories.

7. TIME TO ACT

Now that you've done your research on a news story or fact, it's time to decide what to do with it. If you're convinced that it's factual and well reported, go ahead and use it. You can cite it in a research paper, share it online, or pass along the information to your friends. If you decided that it's not trustworthy, do not share it. If it contains harmful language or imagery, tell a trusted adult immediately.

FAKE NEWS RED FLAGS

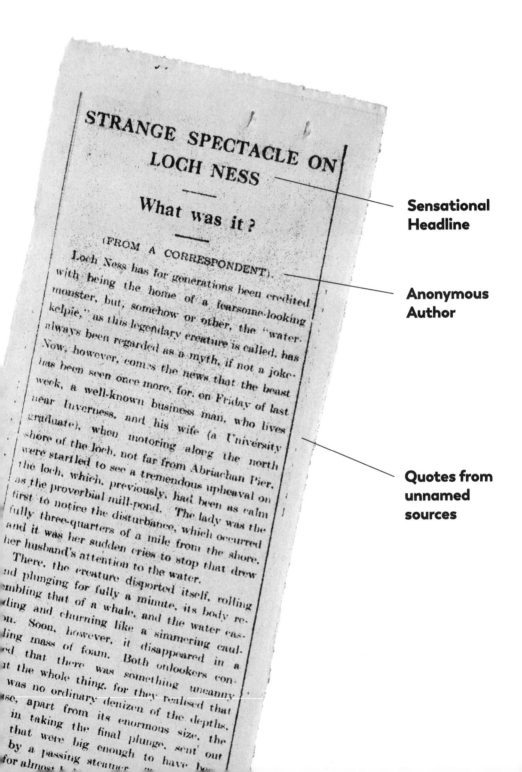

STRANGE SPECTACLE ON LOCH NESS

What was it?

(FROM A CORRESPONDENT).

Loch Ness has for generations been credited with being the home of a fearsome-looking monster, but, somehow or other, the "water-kelpie," as this legendary creature is called, has always been regarded as a myth, if not a joke. Now, however, comes the news that the beast has been seen once more, for, on Friday of last week, a well-known business man, who lives near Inverness, and his wife (a University graduate), when motoring along the north shore of the loch, not far from Abriachan Pier, were startled to see a tremendous upheaval on the loch, which, previously, had been as calm as the proverbial mill-pond. The lady was the first to notice the disturbance, which occurred fully three-quarters of a mile from the shore, and it was her sudden cries to stop that drew her husband's attention to the water.

There, the creature disported itself, rolling and plunging for fully a minute, its body resembling that of a whale, and the water cascading and churning like a simmering cauldron. Soon, however, it disappeared in a boiling mass of foam. Both onlookers confessed that there was something uncanny about the whole thing, for they realised that it was no ordinary denizen of the depths, because, apart from its enormous size, the beast, in taking the final plunge, sent out waves that were big enough to have been caused by a passing steamer.

The watchers waited for almost h...

Sensational Headline

Anonymous Author

Quotes from unnamed sources

ACKNOWLEDGMENTS

To my husband and children, thank you for your patience, enthusiasm, and humor. I promise to stop talking about monsters . . . soon. To the greatest agent there ever was, Jennifer Unter, thank you. I will never stop bragging about the fact that I get to work with you. To my editor, Susan Dobinick, thank you for your collaboration, support, and enthusiasm. Your vision transformed this book into something I'm so proud of. To the many, many experts who helped me along my research journey, thank you. I am especially grateful to the following: Adrian Shine (director of the Loch Ness Project), William Cameron (global ambassador for the Highlands and director of Loch Ness Marketing), Cindy Otis (author and former CIA analyst), Peter Wetherell (descendent of Marmaduke and Ian Wetherell), Steven Smale (Christian Spurling's biographer), Edward Adelson (vision science professor at MIT), Annie Pezalla (psychology professor at Macalester College) Alan Gillespie (former Jet Propulsion Laboratory photo enhancer and professor at University of Washington), and Dick Raynor (Loch Ness Investigation Bureau). Finally, to the librarians and archivists at the British Library, the Inverness Library, and the Lisle Library District, I love you.

SOURCE NOTES

CHAPTER 1: BEGINNINGS

"A most interesting . . . part of the Highlands": Ronald Binns. *The Loch Ness Mystery Solved.*

"very poor and practically dangerous": "The Herring Fishing," *Nairnshire Telegraph*, September 12, 1933.

"Lamentably": Gareth Williams. *A Monstrous Commotion.*

"a correspondent.": "Strange spectacle on Loch Ness: What was it?" *Inverness Courier*, May 1933.

"fearsome-looking": Ibid.

CHAPTER 2: WANDERLUST

"excellent": "Wanderlust," *Era*, April 5, 1933.

"bust up": in "Chatty Gossip of the Day," *Sunday Post*, May 10, 1925.

"Please excuse . . . the cause of art.": Henry Walton. *Livingstone: Fifty Years After.*

"Man of Many Parts": "Chatty Gossip of the Day," *Sunday Post*, May 10, 1925.

CHAPTER 3: MONSTER SIGHTINGS

"beastie": "Loch Ness Mystery 'Monster,'" *Dundee Courier*, May 23, 1933.

"previously disbelieved": Ibid.

"very popular . . . with residents." Gareth Williams. *A Monstrous Commotion.*

"When cruising . . . a camera.": Ibid.

"some distance . . . a heavy body.": "Loch-Ness 'Monster' Seen Again," *Inverness Courier*, June 2, 1933.

"unpleasant and exciting": Nicholas Witchell. *Loch Ness Story.*

CHAPTER 4: ABOMINATION

"quiet": "Are Hunters Closing in on the Loch Ness Monster?" *Scotsman*.com.

"retiring": Nicholas Witchell. *Loch Ness Story.*

"after you": "Are Hunters Closing in on the Loch Ness Monster?" *Scotsman*.com.

"six feet . . . that exists.": "Visitor's Experience Near Foyers," *Inverness Courier*, August 4, 1933.

CHAPTER 5: KONG

"aim is to make . . . all my expectations.": "In the Limelight and Shadow," *Sunday Mirror*, April 3, 1933.

"Not From King Kong's Isle.": "Loch Ness Monster Killed?" *Reynolds's Newspaper*, October 29, 1933.

"lifted right off of *King Kong*'s Skull Island.": Daniel Loxton and Donald R. Prothero. *Abominable Science: Yeti, Nessie, and Other Famous Cryptids*. New York: Columbia University Press, 2013.

"Many people. . . . as facts": Blumer, "Movies and Conduct: 1933," AmericanInClass.com.

CHAPTER 6: SILLY SEASON

"When all . . . arises in his horrendous majesty.": "Thoughts in the Wake of the Sea Serpent," *Chicago Tribune*, December 26, 1933.

"quite as big as a . . . never seen anything like it before.": "Loch Ness Monster Again," *Dundee Courier*, August 9, 1933.

"a big black object . . . of shining rock.": Ronald Binns. *Loch Ness Mystery Solved.*

"wriggly neck . . . as a snake propels itself.": *Dundee Courier*, August 31, 1933.

"great excitement . . . Don't shoot the monster of Loch News.": Anne Morrow Lindbergh, *Locked Rooms and Open Doors.*

"strangely shaped floating object": "Interesting Gleanings from Far and Near," *Hartlepool Northern Daily Mail*, December 13, 1933.

"I am of the opinion . . . a large grey seal": "The Loch Ness Monster," *Dundee Courier*, October 24, 1933.

"may be . . . a horse": "The Loch Ness Monster," *Aberdeen Press and Journal* January 9, 1934.

"improbable or absurd": "Loch Ness Monster," *Aberdeen Press and Journal,* December 18, 1933.

"nothing in the way of . . . abnormal fish or beasts": Ronald Binns. *Loch Ness Mystery Solved.*

"kill a good yarn . . . the beautiful loch.": Gareth Williams. *A Monstrous Commotion.*

"[If] a body . . .": by Henry Lauder, "Ye Lochs and Loons," *John Bull*, December 23, 1933.

"protect the great shoals of salmon": "Loch Ness 'Monster,'" *Edinburgh Evening News*, October 20, 1933.

"dredge": "The Loch Ness Monster," *Falkirk Herald*, December 23, 1933.

"the best silly season of all time": Elizabeth Montgomery Campbell and John Solomon. *Search for Morag.*

"fair game . . . hanged, drawn, and quartered." "Loch Ness 'Monster' Special Act of Parliament Asked for Its Protection," *Falkirk Herald*, November 18, 1933.

"the evidence . . . no law for the for the protection of 'monsters.'" David Clarke. *Britain's X-Traordinary Files.* London: Bloomsbury, 2014, 181.

CHAPTER 7: MONEY

"Would not the Scottish office . . . unemployment in Scotland?": "Doubts About Loch Ness 'Monster,'" *Gloucestershire Echo*, December 12, 1933.

"The bank is something more than men . . . they can't control it.": John Steinbeck. *Grapes of Wrath.*

"New Zealand, Chicago, Siam . . . New Jersey.": "Loch Ness Monster Brings Good Times to Highlands," *Kingston Whig-Standard*, October 19, 1934.

"much amused": "Queen Pays Another Visit to Fair," *Aberdeen Press and Journal*, February 23, 1935.

"They are wondering . . . into Loch Ness.": "Lance's," *Driffield Times*, February 3, 1934.

"I broadcast . . . all over the world.": Ronald Binns. *Loch Ness Mystery Solved.*

"the monster proves to be . . . found in these latitudes.": "Loch Monster on Lloyds," *Daily Telegraph*, December 15, 1933.

"In good health . . . on my hands.": Robert Talley, "Arkansas' Hunt for 'Monster' Hiding in River Bed Recalls Strange Tales of Strange Creatures," *Oklahoma News*, August 8, 1937.

CHAPTER 8: SCIENCE

"All about us . . . bequeathed to us all.": George Matthew Adams, "Today's Talk," *Greenville News*, September 20, 1934.
"In these strange, somber depths . . . creatures out of a nightmare.": David Dietz, "Sea Depths Remind of 'Inferno' and 'Alice in Wonderland,'" *Knoxville News-Sentinel*, August 20, 1934.
"So keen is the modern zoologist . . . or nail of a toe": "Is There a Loch Ness Monster?" *Daily Mail*, January 3, 1934.

CHAPTER 9: PICTURES

"well-known amateur photographer.": Paul Harrison. *Encyclopedia of the Loch Ness Monster*.
"Large box . . . telephoto lens.": Nicholas Witchell. *Loch Ness Story*.
"Vouched for by three responsible persons.": "£100 for a Photo," *London Daily News*, October 24, 1933.
"falling all . . . Loch Ness.": "Monstrous!" *Inverness Courier*, December 19, 1933.
"high naval officer": Frederic J. Haskin, "The Monster of Loch Ness," *Morning Call*, January 20, 1934, 12.
"recognized authority upon marine monsters.": "Scotland Forever," *Province*, January 8, 1935.
"I had hardly sat down . . . above the surface of the water": Daniel Loxton and Donald R. Prothero. *Abominable Science: Yeti, Nessie, and Other Famous Cryptids*.
"I understand that a good picture . . . was seen.": "Tales of Huge Sea Serpents Excite Europe," *Morning Call*, January 20, 1934.
"I was afraid of the chaff . . . upon me": Nicholas Witchell. *Loch Ness Story*.
"utterly unconvincing": "Loch Ness Monster Again!" *Daily Telegraph*, December 6, 1933.
"The Man Who Snapped the Monster." *Aberdeen Press and Journal*, December 9, 1933.
"We don't want . . . in it.": Jonathan Betts. *Harrison Timekeepers and RT Gould, the Man Who Knew (almost) Everything*.
"trail of foam . . . hours": Nicholas Witchell. *Loch Ness Story*.

"certainly a seal": "The Man Who Snapped the Monster," *Aberdeen Press and Journal*, December 9, 1933.

"gigantic sea monster . . . into the air.": "U-Boat Captain's 'Monster' Story," *Daily Telegraph*, December 20, 1933.

"The case of the Monster in the Loch . . . mass hallucination.": "At Loch Ness," *Time*, January 15, 1934.

"the existence . . . for psychologists.": Ibid.

CHAPTER 10: MARMADUKE

"The busy man's paper . . . and home matters.": Fred Arthur McKenzie, *Mystery of the Daily Mail*.

"If you go to Africa, I shall follow.": Adrian Addison. *Mail Men: The Unauthorized Story of the Daily Mail*.

"young, pretty, blonde . . . attention to such details.": "African Jaunt Needs Lady of Many Virtues," *Winnipeg Tribune*, September 2, 1933.

"most influential of England.": "Zoological Gardens and Aquaria," *Boston Evening Transcript*, May 22, 1889.

"funny" and "intelligent.": David Martin and Alastair Boyd. *Nessie: The Surgeon's Photo Exposed*.

"dense.": Daniel Loxton and Donald R. Prothero. *Abominable Science: Yeti, Nessie, and Other Famous Cryptids*.

"The loch . . . mountains.": "Loch Ness 'Monster,'" *Inverness Courier*, December 19, 1933.

"After seeing . . . have completely disappeared": "Organized Search for Monster," *Dundee Evening Telegraph*, December 19, 1933.

CHAPTER 11: THE HUNT

"What is believed . . . see it.": F. W. Memory. "Loch Monster Tracks Found," *Daily Mail*, December 20, 1933.

"where [he] expected.": "Search for Loch ness Monster." *Gloucester Citizen*, December 21, 1933.

"I definitely pledge . . . in Loch Ness.": "Loch Ness Monster: Hunter's Deduction from Tracks Found," *Staffordshire Sentinel*, December 21, 1933.

"The cast . . . of the world.": "Experts Examine Spoor Cast at the Natural History Museum, *Daily Mail*, December 23, 1933.

"eight or nine humps": "The Day's News in Brief," *Aberdeen Press and Journal*, January 1, 1934.

"were very much like . . . the hippo.": "Hunter's Story of Finding Spoor," *Scotsman*, December 26, 1933.

"Here's to the monster. . . . grow less.": "'Monster' of Loch Ness Starts Giant Racket," *Daily Herald*, January 1, 1934.

"We are unable to. . . a hippopotamus.": "Monster Mystery Deepens," *The Daily Mail*, January 4, 1934.

CHAPTER 12: PLOT

"Lochnessity is . . . a gigantic hoax?": "Lochnessity," *Kirriemuir Free Press and Angus Advertiser*, January 11, 1934.

"easily hold . . . goat.": Tony Harmsworth, *Loch Ness Understood*.

"They've swallowed it.": Ronald Binns. *Loch Ness Mystery Solved*.

"a very big . . . doubt": F. W. Memory. "A Very Big Seal," *Daily Mail*, January 16, 1934.

"absolutely convinced . . . deep waters": "Abbot's Theory," *Daily Mail*, January 19, 1934.

"Gutter press . . . can descend": "Mud." *Inverness Courier*, January 9, 1934.

"It just shows . . . an elephant's foot.": "An East Riding Milk Surprise," *Hull Daily Mail*, January 23, 1934.

"You have to choose . . . and us.": "Monsterous," *Reynold's Newspaper*, January 28, 1934.

"All right, . . . their monster.": David Martin and Alastair Boyd, *Nessie: The Surgeon's Photo Exposed*.

CHAPTER 13: HOAX

"but most . . . three elephants.": David Martin and Alastair Boyd. *Nessie: The Surgeon's Photo Exposed*.

"He was a great raconteur . . . amused.": Peter Wetherell, personal interview, July 21, 2022.

"Can you . . . a monster?": David Martin and Alastair Boyd. *Nessie: The Surgeon's Photo Exposed*.

"Well, a monster . . . pleased with it": Ibid.

"We found an inlet . . . in the background.": Daniel Loxton and Donald R. Prothero. *Abominable Science: Yeti, Nessie, and Other Famous Cryptids*.

"R.K. was . . . sense of humor": David Martin and Alastair Boyd. *Nessie: The Surgeon's Photo Exposed*.

"You haven't . . . have you?": Nicholas Witchell. *Loch Ness Story*.

CHAPTER 14: SUCCESS

"a sudden commotion . . . sink from view.": "West End Surgeon's Photo of the Monster," *Daily Mail*, April 21, 1934.

"It was like . . . seen before.": Ibid.

"The Scotch monster . . . sea beasts.": Frank Parker Stockbridge. "Today and Tomorrow," *Opp Weekly News*, May 3, 1934.

"the dorsal fin . . . killer whale.": "Loch Ness 'Monster' May Be a Whale, Claim." *Edmonton Journal*, April 23, 1934.

"May be a diving bird.": "Seeing Not Believing." *Montreal Star*, April 21, 1934.

"Should you . . . welcome.": "Loch Ness Monster: National History Museum plotted to kill creature and display carcass," *BelfastTelegraph.co.uk*, October 28, 2014.

"rights to . . . available.": "Plot to Kidnap Loch Ness Monster Revealed by Sheffield Academic," *Yorkshirepost.co.uk*, October 27, 2014.

"We think . . . beneficent influence.": Ibid.

"thousands of people visited . . . the loch.": Ronald Binns. *Loch Ness Mystery Solved*.

"Inexperienced": Constance Whyte, *More Than a Legend*.

"I am not able . . . submerged": "Loch Ness Monster Seen by London Surgeon Yesterday," *Inverness Courier*, April 20, 1934.

"good-natured fun": "Sea Serpent Hoax of 1904 Is Bared." *New York Times*, April 25, 1934.

"Scots were . . . in like manner": Ibid.

CHAPTER 15: NESSIE

"Only a foolish optimist . . . dark realities of the moment.": President Franklin Delano Roosevelt, inaugural address, 1933.

"Not the fearsome . . . shaped": "The Loch Monster Seen by a Monk," *Sphere*, July 9, 1934.

"The other day . . . Monster.'": "Loch Ness Again!" *Daily Mirror*, April 20, 1934.

"A slender . . . top of the crown.": "Modish Girls to Mimic Scotch Sea Serpent." *Baltimore Sun*, August 30, 1934.

"with weird . . . Loch Ness.'": "Loch Ness Monster." *Aberdeen Press and Journal*, February 13, 1934.

"terrible . . . but amusing": Tom Weaver. *Double Feature Creature Attack: A Monster Merger of Two More Volumes of Classic Interviews*.

"sensational": "This Week on the Screen." *Liverpool Echo*, September 4, 1934.

"larger than . . . colossal success": "Drawing the Crowds." *Liverpool Echo*, March 21, 1934.

"the public likes to be fooled.": "Tricks that Surprise." *St. Louis Post-Dispatch*, June 10, 1888.

"The public appears . . . deceived.": Paul Rutherford. *Adman's Dilemma*, Toronto: University of Toronto Press, 2018.

"monster racket . . . might be caught.": "Hint Seamonster is Tourist Bait," *Spokesman Review*, January 2, 1934.

CHAPTER 16: THEORIES

"Besides, one scientist point out . . . the place to escape": "Experts Disagree Over Monster," *Daily Mail*, April 24, 1934.

"Generally improbable . . . daftness.": Dick Raynor. "Tunnels," *LochNessInvestigation.com*.

"'epidemic' was . . . to the surface.": "Loch Ness Monster, Part 13," *Yowieocalypse.com*.

"wiggling motion": Daniel Loxton and Donald R. Prothero. *Abominable Science: Yeti, Nessie, and Other Famous Cryptids*.

"An awful roar . . . with all speed.": Adamnan, *Life of Saint Columba*.

"dseems to . . . 1,300 years.": David Clarke, *Britain's X-Traordinary Files*.

"Every lake . . . on its verge.": Edward Hulme, *Myth-Land*.

"ascribed to . . . eerie surroundings": "The Loch Ness Monster," *Star Tribune*, February 2, 1934.

"The observers . . . on sale in Inverness.": David Clarke. *Britain's X-Traordinary Files*.

CHAPTER 17: RETREAT

"I might . . . it started to operate.": Nicholas Witchell. *Loch Ness Story*.

"probably a seal": "The Loch Ness 'Monster' Probably a Seal," *Guardian*, October 5, 1934.

CHAPTER 18: WAR

"victims of the Hitler regime . . . neighbouring countries": "Help for the Workers of Germany," *Daily Herald*, July 22, 1933.

"knew that it . . . fighting for her life.": "The Loch Ness Monster," *Dundee Evening Telegraph*, August 18, 1941.

"M. A. Wetherell . . . remembered.": "Long Shots," *Kinematograph Weekly*, March 16, 1939.

"Must confine itself . . . over and over.": Timothy Snyder, "How Hitler Pioneered 'Fake News,'" *NYTimes.com*, October 16, 2019.

"pieces of its . . . west coast of Scotland.: "French Say Loch Ness Monster Strikes Mine," *El Paso Times*, December 28, 1940.

"this was the most . . . a sea-serpent yarn.": "There'll Always Be a Monster in Loch Ness," *San Francisco Examiner*, October 5, 1941.

"in really high spirits. . . . has been killed?": "There'll Always Be a Monster in Loch Ness," *San Francisco Examiner*, October 5, 1941.

"Possibly scarred . . . in London and Coventry": "There'll Always Be a Monster in Loch Ness," *San Francisco Examiner*, October 5, 1941.

"Interesting . . . kept the boys interested.": David Martin and Alastair Boyd. *Nessie: The Surgeon's Photo Exposed*.

CHAPTER 19: FLIPPERS

"twenty-footlong hump . . . Loch Ness": Nicholas Witchell. *Loch Ness Story: The Search for the Loch Ness Monster: One of the World's Most Intriguing Mysteries*.

"Then it started . . . moving down there": Ibid.

"Rines . . . sitting on the bottom.": Gareth Williams. *A Monstrous Commotion*.

"still unexplained . . . inconclusive.": "More Photos of Nessie Taken." *Fort Worth Star-Telegram*, November 2, 1972.

"Maybe.": "O What Could It Be . . . The Famed Loch Nessie?" *Palm Beach Post*, November 3, 1972.

"serpent-like head": Darren Naish. "Photos of the Loch Ness Monster revisited," *ScientificAmerican.com*, July 10, 2013.

"elongated and slim": "Chance to Shoot Nessie Missed." *Aberdeen Press and Journal*, September 3, 1979.

CHAPTER 20: TRUTH

"My father, Marmaduke Wetherell, . . . about five": "Making of a Monster," *Sunday Telegraph*, December 7, 1975.

"fairly accurate": "Loch Ness Perception Tests," *LochNessProject.org*.

"quietly . . . Loch Ness.": Gareth Williams. *A Monstrous Commotion*.

"It's not . . . always has been.": David Martin and Alastair Boyd. *Nessie: The Surgeon's Photo Exposed*.

CHAPTER 21: TODAY

"most powerful arguments . . . that Nessie exists.": "Loch Ness Monster
   Is Again Making Waves." *New York Times.* December 5, 1975.

"Monster experts . . . enquirers after the truth.": Ronald Binns.
   Loch Ness Mystery Solved.

"We need . . . have never before seen.": Dr. June Singer quoted in Jane
   Brody, "Whether or Not a Loch Ness Monster Exists, Belief in
   Such Creatures is Thought to Fill Human Need." *New York Times.*
   July 4, 1976.

"As the human world shrinks . . . or something hidden.": Martin
   Belam, "Scientists to Lead DNA Hunt for Loch Ness Monster,"
   TheGuardian.com. May 23, 2018.

"There is a part of . . . to believe.": Lewis McKenzie, "I yearn to believe
   in the Loch Ness Monster, says Boris Johnson," *UK.Finance.Yahoo.com.*
   September 6, 2019.

"I don't want not to believe.": "Film Makers and Highlanders Pin Hopes
   on Nessie," *Sunday Telegraph*, February 4, 1996.

"At the end of the day . . . the whole of Scotland anyway.": "Loch Ness
   Monster Worth Nearly £41m a Year to Scottish Economy,"
   PressandJournal.co.uk, September 14, 2018.

CHAPTER 22: TIPS

"Nothing can be believed . . . in a newspaper.": Thomas Jefferson,
   "Letter to John Norvell, June 11, 1807."

"did not in fact . . . on the moon.": "Conspiracy Theorist Convinces
   Neil Armstrong Moon Landing Was Faked," *TheOnion.com*,
   August 31, 2009.

"We are sorry for publishing . . . without checking the information.":
   Rhia Chohan, "Bangladeshi Papers Tricked by Moon Landing
   Spoof," *Guardian.com,* September 4, 2009.

BIBLIOGRAPHY

BOOKS AND JOURNALS

Adamnan. *Life of Saint Columba*. Edinburgh: Edmonston and Douglas, 1874.

Addison, Adrian. *Mail Men: The Unauthorized Story of the* Daily Mail. London: Atlantic Books, 2017.

Bambery, Chris. *A People's History of Scotland*. London: Verso Books, 2014.

Barczewski, Stephanie, et al. *Britain since 1688: A Nation in the World*. London: Routledge, 2014.

Betts, Jonathan. *Time Restored*. Oxford: Oxford University Press, 2006.

Binns, Ronald. *The Loch Ness Mystery Solved*. Buffalo, NY: Prometheus, 1984.

Butler, David and Gareth Butler. *British Political Facts*. London: Palgrave Macmillan, 2010.

Campbell, Elizabeth Montgomery and David John Solomon. *The Search for Morag*. London: Tom Stacey, 1972.

Clarke, David. *Britain's X-Traordinary Files*. London: Bloomsbury, 2014.

Curran, James, Anthony Smith, and Pauline Wingate, Eds. *Impacts and Influences*. London: Methuen, 1987.

Emmer, Rick. *Loch Ness Monster: Fact or Fiction?* New York: Chelsea House Publications, 2010.

Fisher, Justin, David Denver, and John Benyon. *Central Debates in British Politics*. London: Longman, 2003.

The Geographical Journal. London: Royal Geographical Society, 1901.

Graves, Robert and Alan Hodge. *The Long Week End: A Social History of Great Britain 1918–1939*. New York: Norton, 1963.

Harmsworth, Tony. *Loch Ness Understood* (self-pub., 2012), Lulu.com.

Harrison, Paul. *The Encyclopaedia of the Loch Ness Monster*. Marlborough, UK: Crowood Press, 2000.

Heim, Susanne and Wolf Gruner, eds. *The Persecution and Murder of the European Jews, 1933–1945; German Reich 1938–August 1939*. Berlin, Germany: De Gruyter, 2019.

Heuvelmans, Bernard. *The Natural History of Hidden Animals*. New York: Routledge, 2007.

Hulme, Edward. *Myth-Land*. Frankfurt: Outlook Verlag, 2020.

Journal of the Northamptonshire Natural History Society and Field Club, Volume XIV. Northampton: Jos. Tebbutt, 1908.

Kallen, Stuart A. *Aliens*. San Diego, CA: ReferencePoint, 2011.

Kuhn, Annette. "Cinema-going in Britain in the 1930s: Report of a Questionnaire Survey." *Historical Journal of Film, Radio and Television*. London: Routledge, 2014.

Lindbergh, Anne Morrow. *Locked Rooms and Open Doors*. New York: Harcourt Brace Jovanovich, 1974.

Lomas, Elizabeth. *Guide to the Archive of Art and Design, Victoria and Albert Museum*. London: Fitzroy Dearborn, 2001.

Loxton, Daniel and Donald R. Prothero. *Abominable Science: Origins of the Yeti, Nessie, and Other Famous Cryptids*. New York: Columbia University Press, 2013.

Lutz, Dick and J. Marie Lutz. *Komodo: The Living Dragon*. Salem, OR: Dimi Press, 1997.

Martin, David and Alastair Boyd. *Nessie: The Surgeon's Photo Exposed*. London: David Martin and Alastair Boyd, 1999.

McKenzie, Fred Arthur. *The Mystery of the Daily Mail: 1896–1921*. London: Associated Newspapers, 1921.

Morton, Ray. *King Kong: The History of a Movie Icon from Fay Wray to Peter Jackson*. New York: Applause Theatre and Cinema Books, 2005.

Newman, Kim and James Marriott. *Horror: The Definitive Companion to the Most Terrifying Movies Ever Made*. London: Carlton Books, 2006.

Proceedings of the Scientific Meetings of the Zoological Society of London for the Year 1872. London: Zoological Society of London: 1872.

Report on the British Press, London: PEP, 1938.

Rutherford, Paul. *The Adman's Dilemma: From Barnum to Trump*. Toronto: University of Toronto Press, 2018.

Stead, Peter. "The People and the Pictures: The British Working Class and Film in the 1930s." *Propaganda, Politics, and Film, 1918–1945*. London: Palgrave Macmillan, 1982.

Steinbeck, John. *Grapes of Wrath*. New York: Viking, 1939.

Walton, Henry. *Livingstone: Fifty Years After.* London: Hutchinson and Co., 1925.

Weaver, Tom. *Double Feature Creature Attack: A Monster Merger of Two More Volumes of Classic Interviews*. Jefferson, NC: McFarland, 2003.

Whyte, Constance. *More than a Legend: The Story of the Loch Ness Monster*. London: Hamish Hamilton, 1961.

Williams, Gareth. *A Monstrous Commotion*. London: Orion, 2017.

Williams, Wendy. *Kraken: The Curious, Exciting, and Slightly Disturbing Science of Squid*. New York: Abrams, 2011.

Witchell, Nicholas. *The Loch Ness Story: The Search for the Loch Ness Monster, One of the World's Most Intriguing Mysteries.* London: Corgi, 1974.

NEWSPAPER AND MAGAZINE ARTICLES

"£100 for a Photo," *London Daily News*, October 24, 1933,

"Abbot's Theory," *Daily Mail*, January 19, 1934, 12.

Adams, George Matthew, "Today's Talk," *Greenville News*, September 20, 1934.

"African Jaunt Needs Lady of Many Virtues," *Winnipeg Tribune*, September 22, 1933.

Agate, James, "The Cinema: King Kong," *Tatler*, April 26, 1933.

"Americans to Hunt Dragons," *Time*, August 25, 1926.

"Are Hunters Closing in on the Loch Ness Monster?" *Scotsman*.com.

"At Loch Ness," *Time*, January 15, 1934.

"Believe It or Not British Sages Have Dubbed Him, 'Bob Ripley, F.R.G.S.,'" *Salt Lake Tribune*, February 22, 1931.

Berman, Eliza, "5 Photos That Show How *King Kong* Revolutionized Movie Special Effects," *Time*, March 9, 2017.

Bigelow, Joe, "King Kong," *Variety*, March 6, 1933.

"Billions of Dwellers in the Ocean's Depths," *Monmouth Inquirer*, March 17, 1932.

"Braintree," *Essex Newsman*, February 17, 1934.

Brody, Jane R., "Whether or Not a Loch Ness Monster Exists, Belief in Such Creatures Is Thought to Fill Human Need," *New York Times*, July 4, 1976.

Burton, Maurice, "The Mystery of Loch Ness," *Illustrated London News*, December 8, 1951.

Cadell, Henry M., "An Odious Ode," *Scotsman*, January 4, 1934.

"Cairds' Highland Show," *Dundee Courier and Advertiser*, June 19, 1933.

"Can you swallow that?" *Nottingham Evening Post*, November 15, 1933.

"Central Restaurant," *Broughty Ferry Guide & Carnoustie Gazette*, January 27, 1934.

"Chance to shoot Nessie missed," *Aberdeen Press and Journal*, September 3, 1979.

Chappell, Connery, "See the Conquering Hero, Kong," *Weekly Dispatch*, April 16, 1933.

"Chatty Gossip of the Day," *Sunday Post*, May 10, 1925.

"Chisholm's," *West Lothian Courier*, December 22, 1933.

Chohan, Rhia, "Bangladeshi papers tricked by moon landing spoof," *Guardian*, September 4, 2009.

"The Cinema: King Kong and the Schoolboy," *Scotsman*, May 9, 1933.

"Danish Premier at Inverness," *Scotsman*, July 6, 1936.

"Day Cruise," *Nairnshire Telegraph*, September 5, 1933.

"The Day's News in Brief," *Aberdeen Press and Journal*, January 1, 1934.

Dietz, David, "Sea Depths Remind of 'Inferno' and 'Alice in Wonderland,'" *Knoxville News-Sentinel*, August 20, 1934.

"Different Brown Bread for Each Day in the Week," *St. Andrews Citizen*, April 21, 1934.

Dixon, Campbell, "Film Producer's African Tour," *Daily Telegraph*, September 22, 1933.

"Doubts About Loch Ness 'Monster,'" *Gloucestershire Echo*, December 12, 1933.

Dorsey, James R., "O What Could It Be . . . The Famed Loch Nessie?" *Palm Beach Post*, November 3, 1972.

Dorsey, James R., "Scientists Photograph Ness Monster," *Times-News*, November 5, 1972.

"Duncan's Hazel Nut Milk Chocolate," *Dundee Evening Telegraph*, April 18, 1934.

"Drawing the Crowds," *Liverpool Echo*, March 21, 1934.

"An East Riding Milk Surprise," *Hull Daily Mail*, January 23, 1934.

Elbein, Asher, "Tasmanian Tigers are Extinct. Why Do People Keep Seeing Them?" *New York Times*, March 10, 2021.

"Entertainments," *Shields News*, December 5, 1933.

"Experts Disagree Over Monster," *Daily Mail*, April 24, 1934, 18.

"Experts Examine Spoor Cast at the Natural History Museum," *Daily Mail*, December 23, 1933.

"Fairy Lights for the Monster," *Daily Mail*, December 23, 1933, 9.

"A Few of Low & Co.'s Cheap Lines," *Nairnshire Telegraph*, April 11, 1933.

"Film makers and Highlanders pin hopes on Nessie," *Sunday Telegraph*, February 4, 1996.

"Flight of the Hunter," *Herald Scotland*, December 3, 2005.

"French Say Loch Ness Monster Strikes Mine," *El Paso Times*, December 28, 1940.

"From the World's Scrap-Book," *Illustrated London News*, April 28, 1934.

"Glimpses of Grampuses," *Scotsman*, September 23, 1933.

"Government Health Work Defended," *Aberdeen Press and Journal*, July 9, 1936.

"The Great Move," *Weekly Dispatch*, April 10, 1927.

"Great Open-Air Swimming Gala," *Nairnshire Telegraph*, July 11, 1933.

"Great Super Film 'Livingstone,'" *Daily Telegraph*, January 21, 1925.

Haskin, Frederic J., "The Monster of Loch Ness," *Allentown Morning Call*, January 20, 1934, 12.

"Help for the Workers of Germany!" *Daily Herald*, July 22, 1933.

Henley, Jon, "Welcome to the newspaper silly season," *Guardian*, August 4, 2010.

"Herr Hitler Enters Prague After His Troops," *Scotsman*, March 16, 1939.

"The Herring Fishing," *Nairnshire Telegraph*, September 12, 1933.

"Hint Sea Monster is Tourist Bait," *Spokesman Review*, January 2, 1934.

"Hip-Hip-O For the Monster," *Reynolds's Illustrated News*. January 21, 1934.

"Hunter's Story of Finding Spoor," *Scotsman*, December 26, 1933.

"I'm Looking for the Loch Ness Monster," *Aberdeen Press and Journal*, January 10, 1934.

"Interesting Gleanings from Far and Near," *Hartlepool Northern Daily Mail*, December 13, 1933.

"Is the Monster a Crocodile?" *Daily Mail*, January 1, 1934, 11.

"Is There a Loch Ness Monster?" *Daily Mail*, January 3, 1934, 8.

"Japanese Interest in Loch Ness Monster," *Scotsman*, January 26, 1934.

"Jokes on 'Invention' of Loch Ness Monster," *Birmingham Gazette*, December 28, 1933.

"*King Kong* Scores Hit in Premiere in Radio City Theatres," *Brooklyn Times Union*, March 3, 1933.

"*King Kong*'s Sensational Premiere," *Kinematograph Weekly*, April 20, 1933.

"Lance's," *Driffield Times*, February 3, 1934.

Latzer, Barry, "Do hard times spark more crime?" *Los Angeles Times*, January 24, 2014.

Lauder, Harry, "Ye Lochs and Loons," *John Bull*, December 23, 1933.

"Loch Monster on Lloyd's," *Daily Telegraph*, December 15, 1933.

"Loch 'Monster' Seen Again," *Dundee Courier and Advertiser*, August 31, 1933.

"The Loch Monster Seen by a Monk," *Sphere*, June 9, 1934.

"Loch Ness Again!" *Daily Mirror*, April 20, 1934.

"Lochnessity," *Kirriemuir Free Press and Angus Advertiser*, January 11, 1934.

"Loch Ness Monster," *Aberdeen Press and Journal*, December 18, 1933.

"Loch Ness Monster," *Aberdeen Press and Journal*, February 13, 1934.

"The Loch Ness Monster," *Aberdeen Press and Journal*, January 9, 1934.

"The Loch Ness Monster," *Dundee Courier and Advertiser*, October 24, 1933.

"The Loch Ness Monster," *Dundee Evening Telegraph*, December 8, 1933.

"The Loch Ness Monster," *Dundee Evening Telegraph*, August 18, 1941.

"Loch Ness 'Monster,'" *Edinburgh Evening News*, October 20, 1933.

"The Loch Ness Monster," *Falkirk Herald*, December 23, 1938.

"The Loch Ness Monster," *Hartlepool Northern Daily Mail*, January 4, 1934.

"Loch Ness 'Monster,'" *Inverness Courier*, December 19, 1933, 5.

"The Loch Ness Monster Is Alive And Well," *Murfreesboro Daily News Journal*, November 1, 1972.

"Loch Ness Monster: National History Museum 'plotted to kill creature and display carcass,'" *Belfast Telegraph*, October 27, 2014.

"The Loch Ness 'Monster' Probably a Seal," *Manchester Guardian*, October 5, 1934.

"Loch Ness Monster. A Suggested Explanation," *Sydney Morning Herald*, September 15, 1934.

"Loch Ness Monster Again," *Dundee Courier and Advertiser*, August 9, 1933.

"Loch Ness 'Monster' Again!" *Daily Telegraph*, December 6, 1933.

"Loch Ness 'Monster' Again Seen," *Aberdeen Press and Journal*, May 23, 1933.

"Loch Ness Monster Brings Good Times to Highlands," *Kingston Whig-Standard*, October 19, 1934.

"Loch Ness Monster: Hunter's Deduction from Tracks Found," *Evening Sentinel*, December 21, 1933.

"Loch Ness 'Monster' Is Blimp's Wreckage," *Bristol Herald Courier*, September 6, 1934.

"Loch Ness 'Monster' Killed?" *Reynolds's Illustrated News*, October 29, 1933.

"Loch Ness 'Monster' May Be a Whale, Claim," *Edmonton Journal*, April 23, 1934.

"Loch Ness 'Monster,'" *Scotsman*, December 14, 1933.

"Loch-Ness 'Monster' Seen Again," *Inverness Courier*, June 2, 1933.

"Loch Ness Monster Seen by London Surgeon Yesterday," *Inverness Courier*, April 20, 1934, 5.

"Loch Ness 'Monster:' Special Act of Parliament Asked for its Protection," *Falkirk Herald*, November 18, 1933.

"The Loch Ness Monster," *Minneapolis Tribune*, February 2, 1934.

"Loch Ness Monster worth nearly £41m a year to Scottish economy," *Press and Journal*, September 14, 2018.

"Loch Ness Mystery 'Monster,'" *Dundee Courier and Advertiser*, May 23, 1933.

"The Loneliest Man in the World," *Sphere*, February 19, 1927.

"Long Shots," *Kinematograph Weekly*, March 16, 1939.

"The Man Who Snapped the Monster," *Aberdeen Press and Journal*, December 9, 1933.

Martin, Douglas, "Robert Rines, Inventor and Monster Hunter, Dies at 87," *New York Times*, November 7, 2009.

Memory, F. W., "Loch Monster Tracks Found," *Daily Mail*, December 20, 1933, 9.

Memory, F. W., "A Very Big Seal," *Daily Mail*, January 16, 1934, 11.

"Memory's," *Middlesex County Times*, May 28, 1932.

"Modish Girls to Mimic Scotch Sea Serpent," *Baltimore Sun*, August 30, 1934.

"The Monster: B.B.C.'s Eye-Witness Account," *Manchester Guardian*, December 18, 1933.

"Monster of Loch Ness," *Gloucester Citizen*, December 22, 1933.

"'Monster' of Loch Ness Starts Giant Racket," *Daily Herald*, January 1, 1934.

"The Monster of White River," *Minneapolis Star Tribune*, August 15, 1937.

"The Monster on the Menu," *Daily News*, January 13, 1934.

"Monster Seen Again," *Dundee Courier and Advertiser*, January 8, 1934.

"Monsterous," *Reynolds's Illustrated News*, January 28, 1934.

"Monstrous!" *Inverness Courier*, December 19, 1933.

Moysey, Stephen P., "Road to Balcombe Street: The IRA Reign of Terror in London, Part I," *Journal of Police Crisis Negotiations*, 8, no. 1 (2008).

"Mud," *Inverness Courier*, January 9, 1934, 4.

Naish, Darren, "Photos of the Loch Ness Monster, revisited," *Scientific American*, July 10, 2013.

"Nature Jotting," *Western Morning News and Daily Gazette*, July 31, 1933.

"New Year's Wishes," *Era*, January 3, 1934.

"Only a Dolphin," *Nottingham Evening Post*, April 26, 1934.

"Organised Search for Monster," *Dundee Evening Telegraph*, December 19, 1933.

"Photograph of Loch Ness 'Monster,'" *Aberdeen Press and Journal*, December 6, 1933.

"Picture Revives Monster Dispute," *Montreal Daily Star*, April 21, 1934.

"Plane Search for 'Monster,'" *Dundee Courier and Advertiser*, December 19, 1933.

"'Plot to kidnap' Loch Ness monster revealed by Sheffield academic," *Yorkshire Post*, October 27, 2014.

Semple, Robert, "Loch Ness Monster Is Again Making Waves," *New York Times*, December 5, 1975.

Siddique, Haroon, "Loch Ness monster: remains of film model discovered by robot," *Guardian*, April 13, 2016.

"Snap £50 To-day," *Weekly Dispatch*, April 15, 1934.

Snyder, Timothy, "How Hitler Pioneered 'Fake News,'" *New York Times*, October 16, 2019.

"St. George's Theatre," *Whitstable Times and Tankerton Press*, July 31, 1926.

"Stage and Screen," *Shields Daily News*, December 24, 1927.

"Stamping Out Disease," *Leicester Evening Mail*, December 20, 1933.

Stockbridge, Frank Parker, "Today and Tomorrow," *Opp Weekly News*, May 3, 1934.

"Strange spectacle on Loch Ness: What was it?" *Inverness Courier*, May 1933.

"Surprise Term Bargains at Cope's," *Nairnshire Telegraph*, December 12, 1933.

"Tales of Huge Sea Serpents Excite Europe," *Allentown Morning Call*, January 20, 1934.

Talley, Robert, "Arkansas' Hunt for 'Monster' Hiding In River Bed Recalls Strange Tales of Strange Creatures," *Oklahoma News*, August 8, 1937.

Taylor, Howard, "The Politics of the Rising Crime Statistics of England and Wales, 1914–1960," *Crime, History & Societies* 2, no. 1 (1998).

"There'll Always Be A Monster in Loch Ness," *San Francisco Examiner*, October 5, 1941.

"Thoughts in the Wake of the Sea Serpent," *Chicago Daily Tribune*, December 26, 1933.

"Tinsel & Sawdust Under the 'Big Top,'" *Western Morning News and Daily Gazette*, January 19, 1938.

Todd, Douglas, "One in four Scots believe Loch Ness 'Monster' real," *Vancouver Sun*, March 2, 2012.

"Tricks that Surprise," *St. Louis Post-Dispatch*, June 10, 1888.

"U-Boat Captain's 'Monster' Story," *Daily Telegraph*, December 20, 1933.

"Value of Seconds," *Weekly Dispatch*, March 27, 1927.

"Visitor's Experience Near Foyers," *Inverness Courier*, August 4, 1933, 5.

"Voice from Sea Depths," *Kansas City Times*, September 23, 1932.

"Wanderlust," *Era*, April 5, 1933.

Webster, Walter, "In the Limelight and Shadow," *Sunday Mirror*, April 16, 1933.

"West End Surgeon's Photo of the Monster," *Daily Mail*, April 21, 1934.

Wetherell, M. A., "Across Africa With a Camera," *Wide World Magazine*, May 1926. 43.

"This Week on the Screen," *Liverpool Echo*, September 4, 1934.

"With Livingstone in Central Africa," *Daily Telegraph*, November 10, 1924.

"Who's Afraid of the Big, Bad African Jungle?" *Omaha Sunday Bee-News*, January 14, 1934.

Woliston, Jack, "Scientist Records Two Monsters in Loch Ness," *Cumberland News*, December 14, 1972.

"W. T. Calman," *Journal of Crustacean Biology* 8, no. 4, October 1, 1988.

"Zoological Gardens and Aquaria," *Boston Evening Transcript*, May 22, 1889

WEBSITES

"9.5mm film—*The Secret of the Loch* SB3017: 1936," YouTube, youtube.com/watch?v = QnuqQ2riunE.

"1939 England and Wales Register for Lilian M Spicer," ancestry.co.uk, ancestry.co.uk/imageviewer/collections/61596/images/tna_r39_0825_0825i_008?usePUB = true&usePUBJs = true&pId = 10590763.

"AFMKY8," alamy.com, alamy.com/nazism-national-socialism-press-newspaper-der-strmer-number-16-nuremberg-image7988983.html.

"The Arms and Tentacles of the Colossal Squid," Museum of New Zealand, tepapa.govt.nz/discover-collections/read-watch-play/science/anatomy-colossal-squid/arms-and-tentacles-colossal.

Bader, Christopher, et al, "American Piety in the 21st Century," Baylor University, September 2006, baylor.edu/content/services/document.php/33304.pdf.

"Bank Holiday of 1933," FederalReserveHistory.org, federalreservehistory.org/essays/bank-holiday-of-1933#: ~ :text = March % 201933, confidence % 20in % 20the % 20financial % 20system.

Blumer, Herbert. "Movies and Conduct: 1933," AmericaInClass.org, americainclass.org/sources/becomingmodern/machine/text6/movies conduct.pdf .

Cannon, H. Graham, "William Thomas Calman," Royal Society Publishing, royalsocietypublishing.org/doi/pdf/10.1098/rsbm.1953.0003.

"Carcharodontosaurus," Western Australia Museum,museum.wa.gov. au/explore/dinosaur-discovery/carcharodontosaurus.

"The Chambers Family of Rosemont," Thornburyroots.co.uk,thornbury roots.co.uk/families/chambers-jt/.

Ciampaglia, Giovanni and Fililppo Menczer, "These are the three types of bias that explain all the fake news, pseudoscience, and other junk in your News Feed," Niemanlab.org, June 20, 2018, niemanlab.org/2018/ 06/these-are-the-three-types-of-bias-that-explain-all-the-fake-news -pseudoscience-and-other-junk-in-your-news-feed/.

"Classic Sightings: Aldie Mackay." *Lochnessmystery.blogspot.com.* April 30, 2013. lochnessmystery.blogspot.com/2013/04/classic-sightings -aldie-mackay.html

"Conspiracy Theorist Convinces Neil Armstrong Moon Landing Was Faked," TheOnion.com, August 31, 2009, theonion.com/conspiracy -theorist-convinces-neil-armstrong-moon-landi-1819570978.

"Context," ColonialFilm.org, colonialfilm.org.uk/node/1844.

"Crime in the Great Depression," History.com, history.com/topics/ great-depression/crime-in-the-great-depression.

"Daily Mail Hat Competition 1920," Shutterstock.com, shutterstock. com/editorial/image-editorial/daily-mail-hat-competition-winner-1920 -mr-albert-owen-hopkins-ao-hopkins-won-the-daily-mail-competition -with-his-design-the-sandringham-hat-picture-shows-albert-hopkins -wearing-the-original-model-of-the-hat-in-1949--882237a.

Dash, Mike, "Baron Von Forstner and the U28 Sea Serpent of 1915," AForteanintheArchives.wordpress.com, January 8, 2010, aforteantinthe archives.wordpress.com/2010/01/08/baron-von-forstner-and-the-u28 -sea-serpent-of-1915/.

"*Der Stürmer*," Holocaustresearchproject.org,holocaustresearchproject. org/holoprelude/dersturmer.html.

"England's Architeuthis," Tonmo.com, February 23, 2020, tonmo.com/ articles/england's-architeuthis.77/.

"The Eyes of the Colossal Squid," Museum of New Zealand, tepapa.govt.nz/discover-collections/read-watch-play/science/anatomy-colossal-squid/eyes-colossal-squid.

"Fake News," University of Virginia, guides.lib.virginia.edu/c.php?g= 600315&p = 4157699.

Field, Clive D., "Loch Ness Monster," British Religion in Numbers, March 25, 2012, brin.ac.uk/loch-ness-monster/.

"Fun Aegyptosaurus Facts." Kidadl.com, kidadl.com/dinosaur-facts/aegyptosaurus-facts.

"History of Unemployment," Scottish Unemployed Workers, scottishunemployedworkers.net/history-of-unemployment.

"History of the London Coliseum," London Coliseum, londoncoliseum.org/your-visit/history-of-the-london-coliseum/.

"Hull New Theater," Broadway World, broadwayworld.com/theatre/Hull-New-Theatre.

Jefferson, Thomas, "Letter to John Norvell, June 11, 1807," Library of Congress, loc.gov/resource/mtj1.038_0592_0594/?sp = 2&st = text.

Jones, Valerie, "People are claiming to have seen the Tasmanian tiger— 80 years after it was believed extinct," *Deseret News*, October 22, 2019, deseret.com/2019/10/22/20926970/tasmanian-tiger-wolf-thylacine-marsupial-extinction-australia-sightings.

Kielty, Martin, "When AC/DC Hunted The Loch Ness Monster," Ultimate Classic Rock, October 28, 2020, ultimateclassicrock.com/acdc-loch-ness-monster/.

Knox, W W, *A History of the Scottish People*, scran.ac.uk/scotland/pdf/SP2_5Income.pdf.

Lee, Steve, "The Original King Kong Armature," Hollywood Lost and Found, December 28, 2005, hollywoodlostandfound.net/props/kingkong.html.

"Loch Ness," *Britannica Online*, britannica.com/place/Loch-Ness-lake-Scotland-United-Kingdom.

"Loch Ness is a giant spirit level," National Oceanography Centre, January 4, 2012, noc.ac.uk/news/loch-ness-giant-spirit-level.

"Loch Ness Monster," Busch Gardens, buschgardens.com/williamsburg/roller-coasters/loch-ness-monster/.

"Loch Ness Monster, Part 13," Yowieocalypse, home.yowieocalypse.com/ Loch_Ness_Monster_13/.

"Loch Ness Perception Tests," Loch Ness Project, lochnessproject.org/ adrian_shine_archiveroom/arcpix/SN93PIX/P14/loch_ness_perception_ test_4htm.htm.

Lotzof, Kerry, "Sea monsters and their inspiration: serpents, mermaids, the kraken and more," Natural History Museum, nhm.ac.uk/discover/ sea-monsters-inspiration-serpents-mermaids-the-kraken.html.

McKenzie, Lewis, "I yearn to believe in the Loch Ness Monster, says Boris Johnson." Yahoo, September 6, 2019, uk.news.yahoo.com/ yearn-believe-loch-ness-monster-111251275.html.

Michlig, John, "Kong Files," KongisKing, kongisking.net/kongfiles/ 052205.html.

"Murdered by Hitler: The Other Austrian Dictator," History.co.uk, history. co.uk/article/engelbert-dollfuss-austrian-dictator-murdered-by-hitler.

Naish, Darren, "The 1972 Loch Ness Monster Flipper Photos," Tetrapod Zoology, tetzoo.com/blog/2020/8/17/loch-ness-monster-flipper-photos.

"Nazi Racial Hygiene," United States Holocaust Memorial Museum, ushmm.org/collections/bibliography/nazi-racial-science.

Newton, Pippa, "A Year in History: 1934," Historic Newspapers, historic-newspapers.com/blog/1934-historical-events/.

Raynor, Dick, "Tunnels," Loch Ness Investigation, lochnessinvestigation. com/tunnels.html.

Roosevelt, Franklin Delano, "Inaugural Address of the President." archives.gov/files/education/lessons/fdr-inaugural/images/address-1.gif.

Roper, Clyde, "Giant Squid," *Smithsonian*, April 2018, ocean.si.edu/ ocean-life/invertebrates/giant-squid.

Ryder, Taryn, "Johnny Depp and 4 Other Celebs Who Believe in Cryptids," Yahoo, January 28, 2015, yahoo.com/entertainment/blogs/celeb-news/ johnny-depp-isn-t-alone--4-other-celebs-who-believe-in-cryptids- 192444027.html.

Sheridan, Peter, "Prince Andrew's Russian blackmail, Hunter Bidens $150B scandal, and the Loch Ness monster in this week's dubious tabloids," BoingBoing.net, boingboing.net/2021/10/08/prince-andrews-russian- blackmail-hunter-bidens-150b-scandal-and-the-lock-ness-monster-in- this-weeks-dubious-tabloids.html.

Singh, Sumit, "The Story of Louis Paulhan's Ground-Breaking London-Manchester Flight in 1910," Simple Flying, April 30, 2022, simpleflying.com/louis-paulhan-london-manchester-flight-1910/.

Smale, Steven D., ed. "About Christian Spurling," Christian Spurling, christian-spurling.art/about/.

Thibodeaux, Wanda, "How Much Does a Live-in Maid Earn Annually?" Pocket Pence, May 13, 2017, pocketpence.co.uk/much-livein-maid-earn-annually-8531545.html.

Treffry, Timothy, "Restoration," *QP Magazine*, 2007. qp.granularit.com/media/38990/Restoration_Rupert_T_Gould.pdf.

Trimarchi, Maria, "Could a squid take down a submarine?" How Stuff Works, animals.howstuffworks.com/marine-life/squid-attack-submarine1.htm.

"Unmasking the Face on Mars," NASA Science, May 23, 2001, science.nasa.gov/science-news/science-at-nasa/2001/ast24may_1.

White, Jeanette, "How Tall King Kong Is in Each of his Films," CBR, January 25, 2021, cbr.com/king-kong-height-every-movie/.

"World War II: 'Wartime Domesday' book showing life in 1939 to be publicly available online," *Independent*, November 2, 2015, independent.co.uk/news/uk/home-news/world-war-ii-wartime-domesday-book-showing-life-in-1939-to-be-made-publicly-available-online-a6717281.html.

INTERVIEWS

Alan Gillespie in discussion with the author, October 25, 2022.
Cindy Otis in discussion with the author, September 20, 2022.
Peter Wetherell in discussion with the author, July 21, 2022 and November 22, 2023.

INDEX

Page numbers in **boldface** refer to images and/or captions.

IMAGE CREDITS

p. 8: Courtesy of Shutterstock; p. 12: Courtesy of Rebecca Siegel; p. 14: Courtesy of Classic Collection 2 / Alamy Stock Photo; p. 16: Courtesy of Shutterstock; p. 17: Courtesy of Pond 5/Curious Iguana, Inc; p. 18: Courtesy of British Newspaper Archive; p. 27: Courtesy of British Newspaper Archive; p. 30: Courtesy of Entertainment Pictures / Alamy Stock Photo; pp. 32-33: Courtesy of Moviestore Collection Ltd / Alamy Stock Photo; p. 42: Courtesy of mauritius images / TopFoto; p. 47: Courtesy of Dundee Courier; p. 55: Courtesy of The Globe and Mail, Inc; p. 61: Chronicle / Alamy Stock Photo; p. 72: Courtesy of *The Scotsman*; p. 74: Courtesy of Pond 5/Curious Iguana, Inc; 77: Courtesy of Pond 5/Curious Iguana, Inc; 81: Courtesy of Rebecca Siegel; 85, top: Courtesy of The Globe and Mail, Inc; bottom: Courtesy of Pond 5/Curious Iguana, Inc; p. 90: Courtesy of Pond 5/Curious Iguana, Inc; p. 91: Courtesy of Flickr.com; p. 93: Courtesy of DMG Media; p. 96: Courtesy of Shutterstock; p. 99: Courtesy of The Globe and Mail, Inc; p. 120: Courtesy of Chronicle / Alamy Stock Photo; p. 137, top and bottom: Courtesy of AAS/LNI; p. 143: Courtesy of The Telegraph